Délices de France

Meat & Poultry

DÉLICES DE FRANCE

MEAT & POULTRY

DINE WITH FRANCE'S MASTER CHEFS

KÖNEMANN

Acknowledgements

We would like to thank the following people and businesses for their valuable contributions to this project:

Baccarat, Paris; Champagne Veuve Clicquot Ponsardin, Reims; Cristallerie de Hartzviller, Hartzviller; Cristallerie Haute-Bretagne, Paris; Établissements Depincé Laiteries Mont-Saint-Michel, Saint-Brice; FCR Porcelaine Daniel Hechter, Paris; Harraca/Roehl Design, Paris; La Verrerie Durobor, Soigny (Belgium); Le Creuset Fonte Émaillée, Fresnoy-le-Grand; Renoleau, Angoulême; Maison Mossler Orfèvre Fabricant, Paris; Manridal, Wasselonne; Moulinex, Bagnolet; Pavillon Christofle, Paris; Porcelaine Lafarge-Limoges, Limoges; Porcelaines Bernardaud, Limoges; Porcelaines de Sologne et Créations Cacharel, Lamotte-Beuvron; Porcelaines Raynaud, Limoges; Rémy & Associés Distribution France, Levallois-Perret; Robert Havilland et C. Parlon, Paris; SCOF, St-Rémy-sur-Durolle; Tupperware, Rueil-Malmaison; Villeroy & Boch, Garges-lès-Gonesse; Zanussi CLV Système, Torcy.

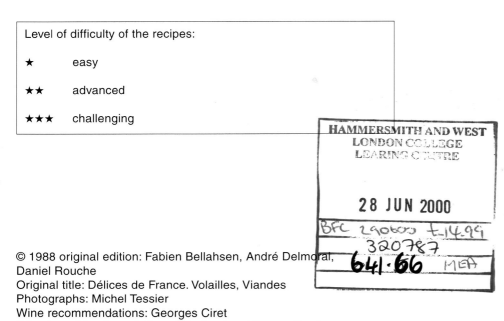

Level of difficulty of the recipes:

★   easy

★★   advanced

★★★   challenging

© 1988 original edition: Fabien Bellahsen, André Delmoral, Daniel Rouche
Original title: Délices de France. Volailles, Viandes
Photographs: Michel Tessier
Wine recommendations: Georges Ciret
(Member of the Association of Professional Sommeliers)

© 1999 for the English edition
Könemann Verlagsgesellschaft mbH
Bonner Straße 126, D-50968 Cologne

Translation from French: Velia Fiori Pryce
English-language editor: Sally Schreiber
Coordination and typesetting: Agents – Producers – Editors, Overath
Reproduction: Reproservice Werner Pees
Production manager: Detlev Schaper
Printing and binding: Leefung Asco Printers, Hong Kong

Printed in China

ISBN 3-8290-2744-3

10 9 8 7 6 5 4 3 2 1

Contents

Foreword

Dining culture is an art that draws people together and fosters harmony. A nation's cuisine is without doubt one of the most important values of any developed civilization, and familiarity with "foreign food" contributes—perhaps even more than we realize—to increased tolerance and mutual understanding between different cultures.

The sixteenth-century French poet Rabelais was well aware of this as he wrote in his novel *Pantagruel*, "Every rational human being who builds a house starts with the kitchen...." And before setting off for the Congress of Vienna in 1815, the French foreign minister Talleyrand reminded his king, Louis XVIII, "Sire, I need pots far more than instructions...."

Thus it is a special pleasure to introduce the *Délices de France* series, a collaborative effort involving many of the preeminent chefs working in France today. Almost 100 masters of their trade are gathered in these comprehensive collections of recipes, representing various geographical regions and branches of the culinary arts that have made French cuisine so renowned: bakers and pastry chefs, chocolatiers, sommeliers, and many more.

All the contributors have already made a name for themselves, or are well on their way to doing so. With its wealth of practical details and background information, *Délices de France* will appeal to anyone with culinary interests—from the hobby cook looking to impress guests at a dinner party to the experienced gourmet interested in improving their craft.

Roger Roucou
1988 President of the *Maîtres Cuisiniers de France*

Chefs' Foreword

For perhaps the first time in history, the *Délices de France* series has gathered the recipes of a large number of well-known chefs in a comprehensive collection of the delicacies of French cuisine. French cooking is revered throughout the world, and we believe that this portion of our cultural heritage, which so greatly enhances the joy and pleasures of life, is one of which we can be proud.

The cookbooks in this series offer a broad panorama of carefully selected culinary delights, and seek to build a bridge between experts from the various gastronomic professions and all friends of fine dining. It gives us, the chefs, the possibility to set down our expertise in writing and to disseminate our professional secrets, thus enriching and furthering the Art of Cooking. Once a luxury, *haute cuisine* is no longer limited to the patrons of elegant restaurants. The recipes presented here range in difficulty from straightforward to quite complex, and are intended to offer you ideas and encouragement in the preparation of your daily meals.

Allow yourself to be inspired! In this collection you will find novelties, acquaint yourself with regional and exotic specialties, and rediscover old favorites. There is a strong continuity between these recipes and the great tradition of French cooking—a rich and varied table offering a broad palette of gourmet pleasures ranging from the simple and light to the extravagant. We have dedicated our lives to this cuisine and are delighted to invite you on this voyage of culinary exploration.

We have made the details in the recipes as clear as possible in order to make it easier to try them at home. In this process, we illustrate our art, which provides a treat both for the palate and for the eye—two pleasures that go hand-in-hand in cooking. With a little practice, you will soon be skilled enough to turn the everyday into the extraordinary, and to impress your guests with culinary masterpieces.

In a special way, the Art of Cooking fosters the social, interpersonal side of life: It is no coincidence that food accompanies all the important milestones of our lives, from a family sitting down together at the table, to holiday celebrations and weddings, to business deals and political meetings.

We are pleased to present you with our most successful creations, so that you can share their pleasures with your loved ones. And we hope that you will have as much fun trying out these recipes as we did creating them.

Furthermore, we hope that the culinary specialties presented in *Délices de France* may serve as an ambassador throughout the world for the enjoyment and pleasures of life, and that this book may in some way contribute both to mutual understanding among cultures and to the refinement of culinary delights.

Good luck in trying out the recipes!
From the chefs of *Délices de France*

Squab

1. Set aside the giblets (hearts, livers, and gizzards) and wrap the birds in strips of pork. In a shallow pan or oven-proof dish containing a little oil and some of the butter, begin roasting the pigeons; take from oven when half-done.

2. Remove the breasts and legs from the birds, and set them aside on a serving platter. Using a meat grinder or food processor, grind up the remainder of the carcasses.

Ingredients:
3 squab or other
    small game birds
3 strips salt pork or
    bacon, blanched
    and drained
2 tbsp oil
6½ tbsp/100 g butter
3 shallots
2 tbsp/30 ml red wine
2 cloves of garlic,
    chopped
1 tbsp tomato paste
1 cube veal bouillon
6½ tbsp/100 ml
    Banyuls
6 slices white bread
1 bouquet garni
salt and pepper

Serves 3
Preparation time: 35 minutes
Cooking time: 40 minutes
Difficulty: ✹ ✹

The word *salmis* is an abbreviation of the lovely word *salmagundis* (English salmagundi) which appears as early as the sixteenth century in the writing of Rabelais, that famed court physician, gastronome, and author, who created Gargantua and his feasts. In culinary terms, *salmis* designates a stew of game birds, particularly the wood dove. Thus we continue to borrow from an ancient gastronomic tradition which has formed the reputation of the finest tables.

If there is no hunter in your family, you can simplify your work by buying game hens that have already been plucked, but make sure their skins exhibit a rosy color. You can easily substitute young pheasants, partridges (quail), grouse, or prairie hens, etc. for the doves, thus widening the possibilities of the recipe.

The strips of salt pork or bacon (blanched first to remove their strong flavor) are important to help keep the fowl tender and protect it from drying out. The giblets incorporated into the sauce give it an unparalleled flavor, so be sure to obtain them from the butcher if you are buying the birds.

This marvelous stew is a classic that has made its way around the world, and your connoisseur friends are sure to enjoy it. The dish loses nothing by being warmed over. Serve it with a delicious purée of celery root, and golden puffed potatoes.

Our wine expert suggests a red Corbières—observe and enjoy the marvelous appearance of this deep and dark wine.

3. To make the sauce, finely chop the shallots and brown them lightly in a pot with a little butter. Pour in the red wine, and cook briefly over low heat.

4. Add the ground carcasses, chopped garlic, bouquet garni, tomato paste, and the bouillon cube dissolved in 2 cups/500 ml water. Grind the hearts, livers and gizzards and add them to the mixture. Season with salt and pepper, and cook gently over low heat for about 20 minutes, stirring occasionally.

Salmis

5. Sprinkle the Banyuls over the reserved breasts and legs. Once the sauce has cooked, strain it into a pan using a fine sieve, and allow it to reduce somewhat over low heat. Correct the seasoning if necessary.
Cut the bread slices into triangles and toast them.

6. Pour the sauce over the pieces of fowl and return them to the oven for about 20 minutes. Remove the birds to the platter and swirl the remaining butter into the sauce. Spoon the sauce over the birds and serve with the toast triangles.

Grandmother

1. Cut the meat into large 1½ in/3-4 cm-cubes. Split the calf's foot and partially bone it. Dice the salt pork; mince the pork rind, and prepare the bouquet garni.

Ingredients:
3 lbs/1.4 kg stewing
   beef
1 calf's foot
3½ oz/100 g salt pork
   or bacon, blanched
3 strips pork rind
4 onions
4 cloves garlic
2 carrots
½ glass olive oil
3 cups/750 ml red
   wine
1 bouquet garni
peel of 1 orange
3 whole cloves
salt and pepper

Serves 6
Preparation time: 20 minutes
Cooking time: 2 hours
Difficulty: ☆

2. Peel the onions and carrots, and cut them into a fine julienne. Mash the garlic, and finely slice the orange peel.

Like good wine, our grandmother's recipes age well, and our chef is well acquainted with this incubation of fine cooking from generation to generation, as the savor improves with time. He shares here a family secret, full of love and tenderness—a recipe that will enliven your meals in the gray season.

Make sure to brown the beef well for this succulent stew before adding the wine. The seared meat will better withstand the cooking process. And since the cooking wine must be very hearty, why not choose a Filou? This regional wine complements the *daube*, or stew, perfectly and adds a country accent to it.

Though simple to make, this dish nevertheless achieves the majesty of the grand tradition of fine gastronomy. Enhanced by the long and patient work of time, this dish will appear regularly at your family gatherings. And your more formal guests will be touched by your sharing with them this traditional delight from "the good old days."

Warmed over, this pot roast will only gain in flavor and aroma, so don't hesitate to prepare it in advance.

Search out a good, well-aged red wine, such as a Minervois from the Domaine de Sainte-Eulalie, to compliment the dish.

3. Bring 2 pots of water to a boil, and blanch the salt pork and rind separately.

4. Place the drained salt pork and rind, the onion, carrots, garlic, and the bouquet garni in a heavy pot with some of the olive oil. Add the orange peel and cloves.

Ascunda's Pot Roast

5. Add the calf's foot and the beef. Mingle all ingredients together well.

6. Pour in the red wine, then season with salt and pepper. Cover and simmer over low heat for 2 hours. Serve hot.

Veal Birds

Ingredients:
12 2-oz/60-g veal cutlets
7 oz/200g sausage meat
3 garlic cloves
3 shallots
7 oz/200g mushrooms
1 egg
10 tbsp/160 ml olive oil
¾ cup/200 ml dry white
  wine
⅔ cup/150 ml veal broth
  (1 boullion cube)
6½ tbsp/100 ml crème
  fraiche
6½ tbsp/100g butter
1 generous lb/500 g fresh
  green pasta noodles
bay leaf
parsley
salt and pepper

Serves 6
Preparation time: 1 hour
Cooking time: 40 minutes
Difficulty: ✩✩

1. For the stuffing, peel the garlic and shallots; mince them along with the parsley. Clean the mushrooms, dice them finely, and add them to the mixture. Gently add the sausage meat and mix well.

Voilà! This recipe is an ever-popular classic, proving itself over and over again. It always fulfills its promise of a delicate and aristrocratic gastronomic experience.

Tightly tied, stuffed and plumped to your taste, these veal "birds" have earned their name precisely because they look like *oiseax sans tête*—little headless birds. It is important that the cutlets be very thin, so if you do not have a meat mallet, ask your butcher to flatten them for you.

The roulades must be well-tied to prevent the stuffing from escaping during the cooking. For best effect, sear them to a golden brown at high heat to give them color, and make sure to serve them very hot. The dish takes well to reheating if you re-warm the sauce first, adding a little water if necessary. Then place the roulades carefully in the liquid, and heat them gently.

These dependable little birds will put you at your ease when entertaining. Serve them with spinach, with pasta (as here), or, more traditionally, on a saffron risotto. Your guests will be delighted with their meal and impressed by your culinary expertise.

The Gamay grape, properly managed, produces red wines full of fruit and charm and always brings out the best in veal dishes. So uncork the bottle and partake of a good Gamay of Touraine (Domaine de Charmoise).

2. Lightly flatten the cutlets. Add an egg to the stuffing, toss lightly, and put a tablespoonful of stuffing on each cutlet. Roll each into a cylinder and tie securely.

3. Season the stuffed "birds" with salt and pepper and brown them in a frying pan with a little oil.

4. Pour the white wine and the veal boullion over the roulades, add the bay leaf, and simmer for about 20 minutes or until done.

with Green Pasta

5. Add the crème fraîche to the pan and simmer gently for a few minutes over very low heat. Remove the roulades to a warm platter and undo the string. For the sauce, strain the liquid through a fine sieve, reduce it somewhat, and whisk in small bits of butter. Set aside.

6. Cook the noodles in boiling salted water. Drain and toss them with the rest of the butter, then place them in a shallow serving dish. Arrange the veal birds on the pasta and serve with the well-heated sauce.

Thighs of Rabbit

1. Brown the rabbit thighs in the oil and 1 tbsp of the butter. Slice the onion and carrot into fairly small pieces, add to the rabbit, and continue to cook. Baste the thighs with mustard, sprinkle with salt and pepper, and add to the pan with the bouquet garni.

2. Pour in the white wine, then stir in the veal broth. Add the unpeeled cloves of garlic to the pan, and cook about 20 minutes over moderate heat.

Ingredients:
4 rabbit thighs
2 tbsp oil
3 tbsp/45 g butter
1 small onion and carrot
1 tbsp Dijon mustard
1 bouquet garni
6½ tbsp/100 ml white wine
¼ cup/60 ml veal broth (1 small boullion cube)
1 head garlic, unpeeled
2 slices/70 g white bread
6½ tbsp/100 ml milk
8 mushroom caps
3½ oz/100 g boiled ham
3 scallions
1 egg
4 small tomatoes; 4 white onions; 1 medium zuchini
salt and pepper

Serves 4
Preparation time: 50 minutes
Cooking time: 55 minutes
Difficulty: ✶✶

In the wonderland of gastronomy, rabbit prepared with unpeeled garlic cloves will surprise no one! Or, if you prefer, substitute choice chicken thighs for the rabbit.

The recipe is simple, but be very careful not to overcook the meat, whose flavor and texture suffer by prolonged heat.

A few more tips to ensure success: Dilute the mustard in a little water before dabbing it on the rabbit so it will not overpower the rest of the ingredients, and be sure to remove the stuffing from the heat before adding the egg to prevent the egg from cooking. Buttering the bottom of the baking dish keeps the stuffed vegetables from sticking.

This dish is to be served very hot, and is an excellent choice for a congenial informal dinner in the country. Leftover rabbit can be kept three days in the refrigerator, but not the accompanying stuffed vegetables. However, you can serve the rabbit cold with a tomato sauce coulis.

Our wine expert suggests you remain in Burgundy where rabbit and mustard are already at home. To add a touch of adventure, she suggests a wine which is unfortunately litte-known: the red Saint-Romain.

3. Remove the thighs to a serving dish and keep warm. Strain the cooking liquid through a fine sieve, bring it to a boil, and whisk in small bits of butter. Remove the garlic and adjust the seasoning if necessary.

4. For the stuffing, soak the bread in the milk and squeeze out the excess. Peel and finely mince 4 mushroom caps, the ham and the scallions. Heat the scallions in some of the butter; add the mushrooms, ham, and finally the bread. Allow the mixture to cook over low heat.

with Whole Garlic

5. Season the stuffing with salt and pepper. Remove it from the heat, add the egg, and mix well. Core the tomatoes, zucchini, white onions, and the remaining mushrooms. Retain the vegetable caps.

6. Fill the prepared vegetables with the stuffing, and cap them. Place them in a buttered casserole, and bake them 15 minutes in a medium oven. Arrange the rabbit thighs and vegetables on a platter, nap with sauce, and garnish with whole garlic cloves. Serve piping hot.

Chicken-Wing

Ingredients:
16 poultry wings
2 shallots
6½ tbsp/100 g butter
4 leeks
2 cups/500 ml red
  wine
2 tbsp oil
salt and pepper

Serves 4
Preparation time: 35 minutes
Cooking time: 30 minutes
Difficulty: ✷✷

1. Remove the wing tips. With a sharp knife, loosen the flesh from the remaining bone and peel it back towards the base of the wing.

2. For the sauce, chop the shallots and brown them in a heavy pot with a little of the butter. Pour in the red wine and simmer slowly until reduced. Add salt and pepper.

Today, fricassée refers to a dish in which the meat is browned in such a way as to bring out all its flavor before it is added to the other ingredients. This chicken-wing fricassée is a good example of the now highly-regarded dish.

The preparation of the wings may seem a little complicated at first. But in fact, all it requires is a scraping back of the flesh toward the base of the bone. After the first try, you will see that it is child's play and the decorative result will add to the charm of the dish. Chicken (or turkey) legs are sold separately and are available all year round. For an interesting variation, try replacing them with veal sweetbreads.

Be sure to mince the leeks finely and watch them carefully while boiling to prevent them from becoming limp. Don't forget to salt the water to keep them green and tender.

The secret of a successful sauce is a perfect reduction. Be patient and don't rush through this step. The wine must be reduced to one-half of its initial volume, thereby giving up its acidity—an important factor in the resulting taste.

This delightful dish goes well with whole spinach, which provides a cheerful companion to the hearty appetites awaiting the fricassée.

Our wine expert suggests a red Saint-Romain. The depth and vigor of this wine from the Côte du Beaune will treat your friends to a pleasant surprise.

3. Wash the leeks carefully and cut them into a fine julienne. Blanch briefly in a pot of boiling salted water. While still crisp, remove them from the pot, plunge them into cold water, and set aside.

4. Strain the sauce through a fine sieve, return it to the pot, and correct the seasoning. Whisk in half the remaining butter in small bits, and set the sauce aside, keeping it warm.

Fricassée

5. In a frying pan, sauté the wings in a little oil over low heat. Season with salt and pepper and turn them from time to time.

6. Meanwhile, sauté the julienned leeks in the rest of the butter. Season with salt and pepper. Place in the middle of the serving plate and arrange the cooked wings around them. Nap with the hot sauce and serve.

Baby Hams of Poultry or

1. Leaving the leg skin in place, bone the thighs along with a generous piece of the flesh. Release the skin around the lower end of the drumsticks to enable it to shrink as the legs plump during cooking. This will add to the desired appearance of the finished dish.

2. To make the stuffing, peel the shallots and chop them finely. Sauté them in butter in a heavy pot. Chop the ham, the livers, and the flesh taken from the legs. Set aside.

Ingredients:
4 chicken legs
l cube chicken bouillon
3½ tbsp/50 ml Noilly vermouth
½ cup/125 ml heavy cream
2 tbsp/30 g butter
1 bunch chives
1 pinch paprika
salt and pepper
For the stuffing:
2 shallots
1 tbsp/15 g butter
1 thick slice boiled ham
3 chicken livers
1 carrot
1 stalk celery
½ cup/125 ml heavy cream

Serves 4
Preparation time: 25 minutes
Cooking time: 35 minutes
Difficulty: ✶✶

The special way in which the poultry legs are stuffed gives this recipe its interesting name—and the dish is as simple as it is distinguished. Both the refined palate of the gourmet as well as the hearty appetite of the gourmand will be tempted by these savory "baby hams." Whatever the season, they will find a place on your menus and rank high among your most privileged recipes.

Make sure you respect the proportions of the stuffing, as this will determine the flavor of the finished dish.

The "baby hams" can be served either hot or cold together with a green bean salad. Or, more elegantly, you might try a ragoût of artichokes or a fricassée of wild mushrooms as an accompaniment.

This dish is at once congenial and unusual, adding fun to your family meals as well as to your fancier get-togethers.

The tender dark flesh of the chicken legs will be piqued by the generous acidity of the Beaujolais vintages. Our wine expert advises a Moulin-à-Vent.

3. Peel the carrot; chop it and the celery very finely, and add them to the shallots.

4. Stir the heavy cream into the sautéing vegetables. When it begins to simmer, add the chopped meats, season with salt and pepper, and cook over low heat.

Stuffed Chicken Legs

5. Let the mixture cool, then stuff the thighs, folding over the skin with its attached flesh to form ham-shaped pieces. Tie securely.

6. Steam the stuffed legs over water 15-20 minutes. Meanwhile, dissolve the bouillon in 2 cups/500 ml water; boil until reduced by half. Add the Noilly and heavy cream and allow to thicken. Beat in the butter in small pieces. Place the chicken on a platter and nap with sauce. Sprinkle with chopped chives and paprika.

Poached Squab with

1. Carefully clean and truss the fowl. Dissolve the bouillon in enough boiling water to cover the birds, and poach the birds in it until tender. Toward the end, sauté the duck liver wrapped in cheese-cloth for 2 minutes. Remove the birds from the broth and set aside.

Ingredients:
4 squab, pigeons, or
  doves
1 lobe fresh duck foie
  gras
1 cube chicken
  bouillon
1 bunch fresh globe
  or pearl onions
⅓ cup/80 g butter
1 bunch chives
1 lemon
1 tbsp sugar
salt and pepper

Serves 4
Preparation time: 40 minutes
Cooking time: 45 minutes
Difficulty: ✶✶

2. Peel the onions, leaving them whole, but removing all but a small piece of the green stem. Brown them lightly in 1 tbsp of butter. Add the sugar and a glass of water to the pan, and cook over low heat until golden and caramelized. Sprinkle with salt and pepper.

The chive onion is a versatile herb. Its showy spiked lavender blossoms make an attractive border around the garden, and in the Renaissance it was used medicinally, especially in the treatment of hemorrhoids. This wild plant that has become at home in our gardens was already known to the ancient Greeks. Wise Athena cites it as indispensable to any cook worthy of the title, and in the French countryside, the herb is known by the evocative name of *appétit*. Doubtless, for this reason the herb is prized in cuisine, especially for flavoring green sauces.

Our chef suggests that you select the squabs with great care. They must have silky feathers and shiny eyes. Guinea hens are an agreeable variant, and may be easier to find in any season.

The preparation of the fowl and the foie gras must be rigorously exact. Make the green chive sauce last so that it still retains its fresh green color when served. This dish goes well with new carrots. Crisp and flavorful, their color and texture will enhance the freshness of the sauce.

Although the recipe requires a certain delicacy of execution, the results well repay the challenge and risks of the enterprise.

With it serve a Savigny-lès-Beaune. You will find the berry-like aromas of this wine to be exceptional.

3. For the sauce, place the chives and the butter in a food processor, and emulsify so as to obtain a chive-butter.

4. Strain half of the squab broth through a fine sieve into a pan, and reduce it by half. Then beat in the chive-butter, a little at a time. Whisk the resulting sauce thoroughly. Add the juice of a lemon and bring briefly to a boil.

Green Onion Sauce

5. Strain the sauce through a fine sieve. Adjust the seasoning. Keep warm but do not allow it to boil.

6. Cut each squab into 4 pieces, bone them, and place them on a serving platter. Slice the foie gras thinly, and arrange the pieces alternately with the candied onions around the birds. Nap with the hot sauce, and serve.

Compote of Leeks

1. Clean the chicken carefully and truss it. In a heavy pan containing water, add the carrots, onion, garlic, bouquet garni and salt and pepper. Add the chicken and poach it for a good hour.

Ingredients:
1 3-lb/1.5-kg chicken
   or
2 chicken breasts
7 oz/200 g carrots
1 onion
3 cloves of garlic
1 bouquet garni
8 leeks
1 cup/250 ml crème
   fraîche
salt and pepper

Serves 4
Preparation time: 20 minutes
Cooking time: 1 hour 20 minutes
Difficulty: ✶

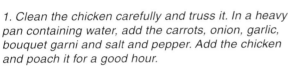

2. Mince the leeks very finely, salt them and let them sweat over low heat. After several minutes add the crème fraîche and continue to cook over a low flame.

True cooks know the art of preparing leftovers. So this recipe is a real blessing! This gratin of leeks allows a lot of freedom. In fact you can add add mild ham, the remains of a stew, mussels, smoked salmon.... the variations are almost endless. In addition, the leek is rich in fibers and known for its diuretic properties.

Leeks soften with no need of additional fat. Just cover them with aluminum foil so they sweat or steam over a low heat.. Be careful! They must not color up or they will add a bitter taste to your dish. Cook them over a low flame for only about ten minutes.

Cooking the chicken takes a bit longer, but it can be done in advance.

This recipe, original and economical, is a real treat. It is right for any occasion and will be sure to please every palate.

Our wine steward suggests a Savennières. The delicacy and finesse of this white wine from the Anjou will be perfect with the vegetal flavor of this preparation.

3. When the chicken is done, remove the breasts.

4. Cut the breast-tenders (the inner muscle that lies next to the breastbone) into very thin slices and dice the rest of the breast meat.

with Chicken Breasts

5. Add the chopped breast meat to the leeks, mix well, adjust the seasoning again and allow to cook for 5 or 10 minutes longer.

6. When serving, prepare individual portions or use a large serving platter. Arrange the tenders on the leek mixture and add a spoonful of crème fraîche. Place the platter briefly under the broiler until lightly golden. Serve very hot.

Osso Buco or

1. Peel and finely chop the onions, shallots, garlic, and carrots.

Ingredients:
1 veal shank, about
    2.2 lbs/1 kg
2 tbsp flour
1 generous lb/500 g
    carrots
7 oz/200 g onions
3½ oz/100 g shallots
3 cloves garlic
1 bouquet garni
2 tbsp/30 ml oil
zest of 1 lemon
zest of 1 orange
1 cup/250 ml white
    pineau
salt and pepper

Serves 6
Preparation time: 35 minutes
Cooking time: 1 hour 30 minutes
Difficulty: ✫

2. Cut the shank into thick slices as for osso bucco, or have the butcher do it. Dredge each piece well in flour.

The pineau of Charentes is a fortified wine which has been produced in the region of Cognac since at least the days of Francis I, the architect of the French Renaissance who brought Leonardo da Vinci to his château in Amboise. Containing 16-20 percent alcohol, pineau may be either white or red, and can be served as an apéritif with melon or foie gras, and enters gracefully into several culinary preparations.

Contrary to the traditional osso buco with its rather acidic tomato overtones, this dish draws upon the sweetness of new carrots, caramelized onions, and pineau to develop its deliciously unexpected flavor.

Our chef favors light cuisine, so he prefers to sweat the vegetables rather than using even the least amount of fat. Cook them over a very low flame, stirring constantly. When they just begin to become tender—but before they become soft—add them to the veal.

Remaining faithful to our chef's principle of reducing fatty elements, discard the cooking liquid and de-grease the pan in which the meat was cooked.

Like all rustic cooking, this dish is very economical. Richly flavorful in the tradition of long-simmered country dishes, this presentation of veal will nevertheless allow you to thrill the most distinguished diners.

To remain the true regional note of the dish, serve it with a well-chilled white pineau, or a red one, if you prefer. If you wish to range further afield, our wine expert suggests a Tokay d'Alsace.

3. In a heavy pot, sweat all the vegetables along with the bouquet garni.

4. Meanwhile, in a second pot, sauté the slices of shank in a little oil until golden. Season with salt and pepper.

Veal Shank with Pineau

5. Pour in the pineau, flambé it, then add enough water to half cover the meat. Cook for 15 minutes over low heat.

6. Deglaze the pan, if desired, and add the vegetables to it, then sprinkle with salt and pepper. Toss all together and allow to simmer gently for 40 minutes. Garnish with a few sprigs of parsley and serve piping hot.

Roasted Legs of

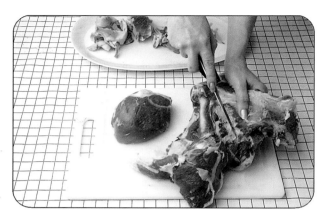

Ingredients:
1 leg of lamb
2 egg whites
2 cloves garlic
several sprigs Italian
  flat parsley
6½ tbsp/100ml heavy
  cream
2 tbsp oil
1 cube beef bouillon
salt and pepper

1. Completely bone the leg of lamb and divide it into 7 pieces. Slit a pocket for the stuffing into 6 of them. From the seventh piece, cut 6 slices of meat to serve as a cover for the pockets of the 6 "lamb roasts."

Serves 6
Preparation time: 25 minutes
Cooking time: 20 minutes
Difficulty: ✫

2. For the stuffing, grind all remaining pieces of lamb using a food mill or processor.

A tiny leg of lamb of one's very own—this is what our chef offers us in this original recipe. Presenting every guest with their own leg of lamb is not only a culinary delight, but in an individualistic age, makes a statement to get conversation rolling.

After removing all excess fat, the original leg must be boned. Carefully follow the contours of the lamb muscles so as to avoid cutting into the meat, thus causing juices to be lost. Except for the muscles next to the bone itself, the muscle tissue will come away cleanly without the use of a knife.

Remove the nerve fibers from the leg and divide it into 6 square portions of flesh which will become the miniature lamb legs. After stuffing them, tie loosely with string so that a single snip will release each packet when it is ready to be served. To avoid overcooking the stuffing, make sure it is well-enveloped in the meat. Serve the miniature legs hot with a garnish of carrots, and green or yellow string beans as the vegetable accompaniment. This dish is both modern and practical. The tedious days of tending a large gigot in the oven are over! This version can be made ahead of time and reheated for exactly 20 minutes before serving. However, it does not take well to reheating again. Instead, thinly slice any leftover "legs" and serve with mayonnaise as a delicious cold repast.

Our wine expert makes a classical choice: a Château Pontet-Canet (Pauillac). The wedding of flavors will make a sumptuous feast indeed.

3. Fold in the egg whites, garlic and half of the parsley. Blend briefly. Season with salt and pepper.

4. Add the cream and blend again to emulsify the ingredients. This completes the stuffing mixture.

Lamb in Miniature

5. Pack a generous tablespoon of the stuffing into the slit of each of the "roasts," and use the extra 6 slices to seal the cavity. Tie each "leg" into a firm, but not overly tight, bundle.

6. Heat the oil in a baking dish, salt and pepper the meat and roast until tender, basting occasionally with pan juices. Remove from the oven and keep warm. Degrease the roasting pan and deglaze with the bouillon dissolved in 3/4 cup/200 ml water. Bring to a boil. Add the remaining parsley and serve with the legs of lamb.

Stuffed Rabbit

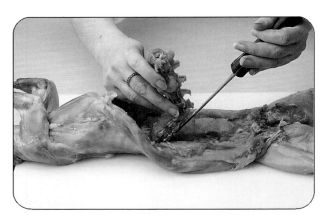

1. Bone the rabbit, being careful not to pierce the skin.

Ingredients:
1 3¼-lb/1.5 kg rabbit
10½ oz/300g pork
3½ oz/100 g veal
1 rabbit liver
2 carrots
2 turnips
1 stalk celery
2 eggs
3½ tbsp/50 ml cognac
6½ tsp/100 ml white
  wine
1¼ cup/300 ml crème
  fraîche
l generous lb/500 g puff
  pastry (see basic
  recipe)
1 tbsp mustard
salt and pepper

Serves 6
Preparation time: 1 hour 10 minutes
Cooking time: 1 hour
Difficulty: ✶✶✶

2. For the stuffing, chop the pork, veal and liver with a food processor or by hand. Pare and dice the vegetables finely.

Here is a rustic recipe for the hunting season that will take the chill off wintry days.

The chef recommends that the animal be extremely fresh with a shiny, clean appearance. Truss the rabbit up firmly and wrap it in a layer of pork fat or a caul, available from the butcher, to keep it from drying out during cooking.

After roasting, let the rabbit cool down completely before placing it in the puff pastry to prevent the dough from becoming soggy.

Although mustard sauce is a perfect complement for rabbit, a brown sauce is also quite acceptable. Armagnac, marc, or any brandy can be substituted for the cognac.

The addition of mushrooms to the stuffing will make this dish even more impressive, or you might add a creative touch by placing pastry cut-outs in various shapes on the surface of the dough before baking.

Serve the baked rabbit-in-crust hot along with steamed potatoes, cabbage, or tomatoes. This dish can also be enjoyed cold, after discarding the pastry shell.

Such rustic culinary fare will please just about everyone and can be the centerpiece of a country buffet.

Our wine-expert advises a Chablis Fourchaumes. The lively, acerbic character of this great wine will bring out the harmony between the delicate meat and the rich pastry wrapping.

3. Blanch the vegetables and set them aside. Toss the meats together with one of the eggs. Add salt and pepper, pour in the cognac, and mix all together thoroughly.

4. Combine the meat mixture with the vegetables until it has a uniform consistency. Stuff the rabbit with the preparation and sew it up using a trussing needle.

in Pastry Crust

5. Sprinkle with salt and pepper. Roast the rabbit, being careful to avoid breaking the skin. Remove it from the oven and let it cool uncovered. Deglaze the roasting pan with the white wine. Whisk while reducing the liquid, add the crème fraîche, and whisk again. Strain the sauce through a sieve.

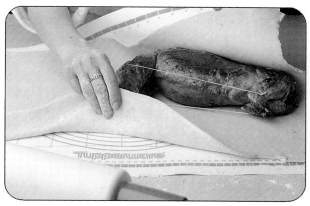

6. When the meat is completely cooled, wrap it in the puff pastry. Glaze with beaten egg and bake in a medium oven for 20 minutes. Add the mustard to the sauce, adjust the seasoning, and serve it with the roasted rabbit.

Chicken in

1. Clean the chicken and cut into 8 pieces. Sauté in some of the butter in a heavy pan until tender. Season with salt and pepper.

Ingredients:
1 2½ lb/1.2 kg chicken
3½ tbsp/50 g butter
3 shallots
3 tomatoes, cored and seeded
½ glass wine vinegar
2 cups/500 ml table wine
2 cups/500 ml meat stock (see basic recipe)
1 bunch chives
salt and pepper

Serves 5
Preparation time: 15 minutes
Cooking time: 35 minutes
Difficulty: ✶

2. Chop the shallots finely, and dice the tomatoes.

Let's forget the traditional boring roasted Sunday chicken! Here's an original way to prepare poultry—and yet it requires no special effort.

But be sure to choose a good free-range chicken, and roast it slowly to let it produce its own juice. In the end, the sauce should not be too thick; to attain the right consistency, reduce the liquid by half once with vinegar, and then again with wine. At the last minute beat in butter in small bits and the trick is done: You will have a perfect gravy.

For the finishing touch, strew chopped chives, or minced chervil and parsley, over the platter containing the chicken.

Along with the chicken, you might serve Creole rice as the recipe indicates, or perhaps turn to the reliable stand-bys of new potatoes or creamed spinach.

This dish is not only simple and succulent, but dietetically sound with its acidic herbal character. You will experience how easy it is to celebrate cherished traditions and still continue to please.

The acidity of the sauce suggests a wine that tends in the same direction, but brings a fruity undertone to round out the ensemble: a Chiroubles.

3. Add the shallots to the chicken and allow to sweat 2 to 4 minutes.

4. Remove the chicken and keep warm. Deglaze the pot with the vinegar, and reduce the sauce 2 to 3 minutes.

Wine Vinegar

5. Pour in the red wine and cook for 5 minutes. Add the meat stock and allow to simmer for an additional 5 minutes.

6. Add the tomatoes to the sauce and adjust the seasoning if necessary. Whisk in the butter in small pieces. Pour the sauce over the chicken, and sprinkle with chives (chervil or parsley). Serve the poulet au vinaigre very hot with Creole rice in tomato cups.

Spring Chicken

1. Cut each bird in half, remove the rib cages, and set aside. Make sure to remove all the skin. Cut the foie gras into 4 slices.

Ingredients:
2 spring chickens
3½ oz/100 g fresh
   foie gras
1 onion
1 carrot
2 tbsp/30 g butter
1 head Savoy
   cabbage
flour for dredging
l generous lb/500 g
   puff pastry (see
   basic recipe)
1 egg white
a pinch of thyme
bay leaf
salt and pepper

Serves 4
Preparation time: 40 minutes
Cooking time: 1 hour 30 minutes
Difficulty: ✳✳

2. Mince the onion and carrot and sauté them in butter in a heavy pot. Cut the cabbage into 4 pieces and lay them on top. Add the herbs, salt and pepper, and 2 cups/500 ml water. Allow the mixture to simmer slowly.

True masterpieces stand up serenely to the test of time. Here is a noble classic which, despite the years, continues to delight on every occasion. The secret of its long-standing popularity lies no doubt in its ability to remain universally pleasing.

The core of success in this recipe lies in the braising of the cabbage, which must be blanched first to make it more digestible. Then sauté the cabbage in oil, or better yet, in the butter in which the onions and carrots have cooked, and add a piece of pork rind or smoked ham. Cabbage likes long braising because it needs time to absorb various flavors and aromas. A good hour's cooking will do wonders for this vegetable. Never be afraid to overcook cabbage. Well braised, it will keep three or four days and can be served with cold meats to make a treat for the family.

Pigeons, pheasants, partridges, guinea or Cornish hens will also make festive fare if you wish to substitute them for the chicken.

You can use the leftover bits of dough to decorate the pastry with leaf or flower shapes or any other form that strikes your fancy.

Our wine expert has chosen a good red wine from the Rhône valley, Crozes-Hermitage, a wine which is also one of the best values in France.

3. Dredge the foie gras slices in flour and fry them in a non-stick frying pan. Season with salt and pepper.

4. Roll out the pastry and cut out 8 circles with a diameter of 6 in/15 cm. Mix a little water with egg white to brush the edges and surface of the pastry and set aside.

in Puff Pastry

5. Once the cabbage is cooked, let it cool. Put about 1 tablespoon of the cabbage on each pastry round and lay a slice of the fried foie gras on top.

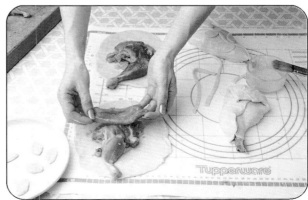

6. Place half a hen atop the cabbage and foie gras and brush the edge of the pastry with the egg mixture. Cover with another circle of pastry, and brush its surface with egg white as well. Fold the top and bottom together and seal well to make a free-form pie. Bake for 30 minutes in a hot oven.

Sautéed Chicken

Ingredients:
1 chicken
⅓ cup/80 ml oil
3½ tbsp/50 g butter
1 head garlic
3 tomatoes
1 glass white wine
1 chicken bouillon
   cube
3 sprigs of parsley
salt and pepper

1. If necessary, singe the chicken and remove the entrails. Divide it into 8 pieces. In a heavy kettle, brown the portions in oil and a little butter.

Serves 4
Preparation time: 30 minutes
Cooking time: 30 minutes
Difficulty: ✶

2. Separate the garlic cloves from the head and remove the outer skins. Add these semi-peeled cloves to the pan and continue browning.

Whether for a master chef or for an amateur, the sky is the limit! Here, our chef from the luxury liner *Ile de France* re-invents a regional favorite. Simple, quick, and unpretentious, this gently sautéed dish will delight your family. Especially light, it is perfect for summer evenings.

Begin by browning the pieces of chicken until they are a deep golden color. This will allow you to collect all the juices which become the heart of its very flavorful sauce. To add the finishing touch to this delectable gravy, whisk the butter into the hot liquid bit by bit just before serving.

The most appropriate garnish, if you wish to stay with the style and spirit of the dish, is *pomme château*—but fried potatoes would be an admirable choice as well. Similarly, you may select some other kind of poultry, as this culinary approach lends itself to a wide gamut of possibilities.

This is just the sort of dish we love both to cook and to eat; furthermore, it does not suffer from being reheated. Chicken is easy to handle and economical. So take advantage of it, dress it up, and show your guests how one can make a fancy treat out of a simple food. The recommended wine is a Seyssel: Its discreet bubbles will transport you in one fell swoop to the heart of the French Alps, to the Isère, where fine cuisine is appreciated.

3. Peel the tomatoes, cut them in half, and seed them. Crush them and add to the pot. Continue cooking.

4. Pour off the fat and add the white wine. Cover and cook slowly for 20 minutes. Salt and pepper lightly.

Grenobloise

5. Dissolve the bouillon cube in 6½ tbsp/100 ml water and bring it to a boil. Remove the pieces of chicken to a warm place, and stir the broth into the kettle.

6. Just before serving, whisk the butter into the hot liquid bit by bit; nap the chicken with the sauce and sprinkle the chopped parsley over all. Serve very hot.

Beef Sirloin with

1. Season the sirloin pieces with salt and pepper. Heat a heavy frying pan and add the oil and garlic. Sear the meat on both sides. Reduce the heat and brown the meat as desired. Remove it and set aside, loosely covered, to gather its juices.

Ingredients:
2 lbs/900 g beef
  sirloin or strip sirloin
2 tbsp/30 ml oil
2 cloves garlic
2 shallots
1 tbsp Dijon mustard
6½ tbsp/100 ml white
  wine
⅔ cup/150 ml crème
  fraîche
3½ tbsp/50 g butter
watercress to garnish
salt and pepper

Serves 4
Preparation time: 10 minutes
Cooking time: 15 minutes
Difficulty: ✯

2. Peel and chop the shallots finely. Toss them in the pan and gently fry until they turn just golden.

The culture of gastronomy has its great classics which have survived through the ages without showing the least sign of age. They give us the confidence and serenity to attempt unusual culinary innovations such as this.

Beef sirloin in mustard sauce is one of those prestigious and immortal gastronomic treasures that must be re-visited from time to time. But prestige alone is not enough to allow a dish to earn the right to join the lofty hall of fame of culinary art. A personal link must be woven between the taster and the tasted, and no one has ever been able to formulate this connection in a recipe. So we continue to innovate.

For best results, our chef advises that the meat first be seared quickly and thoroughly, and that the cooking then be stopped or slowed down until precisely the desired degree of doneness is achieved.

The strength of the mustard is left to your discretion. If you prefer, the amount of sauce may also be increased. This same sharp sauce lends itself well to saddle of rabbit.

It is nice from time to time to have recourse to old habits and tastes, and connoisseurs of red meat will really be delighted by this simple and yet grandiose standby.

In order to meld the rich pulpiness of the beef agreeably with the piquancy of the mustard, our wine expert advises a Morgon.

3. Add the mustard and stir it lightly until well incorporated.

4. Pour in the wine, and stir until it is well blended.

Mustard Sauce

5. Add the crème fraîche and let the mixture simmer briefly over low heat.

6. Strain the sauce through a fine sieve and adjust the seasoning. Finish it by whisking in the butter a piece at a time. Nap the bottom of the warmed serving dish with the gravy. Slice the beef and lay it on the sauce. Arrange the watercress on the platter, and serve.

Veal Medallions

1. Trim the fillet and cut 4 medallions from it. Dredge them with flour and sear them in a frying pan with some of the butter. Remove the veal from the pan.

Ingredients:
4 servings of fillet of
  veal
2 tbsp flour
6½ tbsp/100 g butter
4 shallots
¾ cup/200 ml Banyuls
1 cube veal bouillon
⅔ cup/150 ml crème
  fraîche
1¾ lb/800 g chanterelle
  mushrooms
salt and pepper

Serves 4
Preparation time: 35 minutes
Cooking time: 30 minutes
Difficulty: ✶

2. Chop the shallots finely. In the pan used for the veal, fry up the veal trimmings, add the shallots, and sauté until golden.

Fillet of veal is a real gem in the crown of haute cuisine, due to both its round or oval form and especially its tenderness.

Veal requires great care in cooking, and will need your constant attention. Sear the meat at the beginning to prevent it from drying out. It is important, however, to make sure the meat stays rosy in the center.

During the cooking, add some scraps of fat from the veal to increase the flavor of the resulting sauce.

Sauté the chanterelles after washing them well. Certain cooks prefer to blanch them before frying them in butter, but our chef discourages this practice, as he believes the flavor these magnificent golden trumpets are diminished by such treatment.

Neither the dish nor your guests like to be kept waiting, so be sure to serve the medallions promptly, while they are still hot from the pan.

Rich, solid, sumptuous, veal medallions will unfailingly impress the most discerning and refined of palates.

If you like to follow directions to the letter, you will serve a Banyuls Grand Cru. But if you want to be a bit bolder, try a fine vintage from among the Côtes-du-Rhône or a good Châteuneuf-du-Pape.

3. Pour off the fat and deglaze the pan with the Banyuls. Allow to simmer gently for a few minutes.

4. Dissolve the bouillon cube in 6½ tbsp/100 ml water. Add this to the frying pan, and allow the liquid to reduce for a few minutes longer.

with Banyuls

5. Blend in the crème fraîche and allow it to thicken over low heat. Strain the sauce through a fine sieve. Keep warm.

6. In another pan, sauté the chanterelles in a little butter. Add salt and pepper. While they are cooking, whisk the rest of the butter into the hot sauce bit by bit, off the heat. Place the medallions on a serving platter. Nap them with sauce and surround with the sautéed chanterelles. Serve immediately.

Poached Breast of Veal

1. For the stuffing, chop the liver, parsley, onion and the garlic. Combine this dice with the sausage meat, add the eggs and mix everything thoroughly.

Ingredients:

1 2-lb/900-g veal breast
1 3/4 oz/50 g veal liver
4 sprigs of parsley
1 onion
1 clove of garlic
7 oz/200 g sausage meat
2 eggs
1 handful fresh bread
  crumbs
1 glass milk
3 carrots
3½ oz/100 g French beans
1¾ oz/50 g young peas
1 glass white wine
1 onion studded with 3
  cloves
1 bouquet garni
1 potato
salt and pepper

Serves 6
Preparation time: 1 hour
Cooking time: 1 hour 30 minutes
Difficulty: ✶✶

2. Soak the bread in the milk and pass it through a vegetable mill. Add it to the stuffing. Season with salt and pepper.

A generous veal breast with a plump stuffing hidden inside it—what a treat for the whole troupe! This is a dish that will take care of all appetites, large and small.

Ask your butcher for a boned breast, preferably from the flank end. Using a sharp knife and your fingers open up a large pocket and fill it very full with this hearty stuffing to which you have added egg to hold the elements together.

To make attractive slices, allow the meat to cool down for half an hour before slicing.

If veal is unavailable, try this recipe with a shoulder of lamb. But in that case several additional cloves of garlic will be needed to enhance the flavor of the meat.

Very fresh vegetables will contribute both their flavor and their color to the dish, so be creative with the light and deep green tints of the peas and green beans, the orange of the carrots, the pearly pink transparency of the onions. Let spring dance gaily on the platter! This feast, served tepid, also lends itself to the cool seasons of autumn or winter, when warmed by a hearty accompaniment of steamed cabbage.

Cold, it will keep two days in the refrigerator and will honor a summer banquet alongside a salad lovingly dressed in a vinaigrette made with hazelnut oil.

For the wine, the subtlety and accommodation of the veal will combine well with the delicate fruitiness of a white Beaujolais.

3. Bone the breast if it has not been prepared by the butcher. Separate the 2 main layers of tissue, opening up a pocket within the meat. In 3 separate saucepans, poach 2 sliced carrots, the green beans, and the peas. Monitor each to prevent over-cooking.

4. Drain the vegetables and divide in half. Dice one half of each vegetable finely, and add to the stuffing mixture. Combine all ingredients well by tossing lightly, making sure that the vegetables are not crushed. Using a large serving spoon, fill the cavity of the breast.

with Spring Vegetables

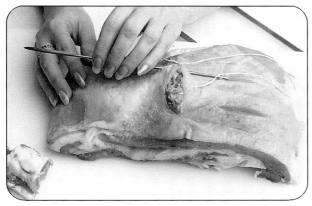

5. Sew up the breast cavity with a larding needle and culinary thread. For the court-bouillon, add the glass of wine, studded onion, bouquet garni, remaining carrot and pepper to a pot of salted water. Bring to a boil.

6. Place the veal breast in the hot bouillon, and simmer very gently for about an hour and a half. In the last half hour of cooking, add the potato. Allow the meat to cool somewhat, then slice and arrange on a platter surrounded by the remaining spring vegetables.

Old-Fashioned Pot

1. Cut the pork fat into strips. Set them briefly in the freezer so they will be firm. Cut deep incisions in the roast with a sharp knife, and wedge the pieces of pork into the spaces.

2. Cut 1 carrot, the onion, and the celery stalk into a fine dice. Prepare the bouquet garni. In a heavy kettle, heat the oil and brown the meat well on all sides. Add the diced vegetables.

3. Once the vegetables begin to color up, add the bouquet garni. Crush and seed the tomatoes, and add them as well. Cook briefly.

Ingredients:
4½ lbs/2 kg beef round
1 piece salt pork
4 carrots
1 onion
1 stalk celery
3 tbsp cooking oil
3 tomatoes
1 bottle Bordeaux
1 glass of port
1 cube chicken bouillon
3 turnips
4 potatoes
2¾ oz/80 g pearl onions
1 tbsp potato flour
1 bouquet garni
salt and pepper

Serves 6
Preparation time: 20 minutes
Cooking time: 2 hours
Difficulty: ✶

This is a one of those old-fashioned dishes that our grandmothers liked to let simmer on a wood fire for hours. If you want to confirm the modernity of old-time recipes, choose this one.

It is crucial that the meat simmer for a long time over low heat. This careful cooking will allow it to become tender and succulent. Our chef suggests you ask your butcher for well-aged meat, so that it will be more tender to begin with.

Sauté the diced vegetables just until they start to turn color in order to prevent the least bit of bitterness from marring the subtle flavor of this dish.

Port wine in the preparation tempers the acidic undertones of the Bordeaux.

To blend and finish the gravy, use potato flour rather than corn starch: Its texture will add a subtle brilliance to the sauce. But take care with the proportions in order to control the liquidity of the resulting sauce.

This country recipe suggests wood fires and snug evenings by the hearth. Or turn to it to shake off the grayness of a rainy night in the city. The voluptuous aromas produced in the preparation of this dish will fill the entire house with warmth.

Our wine choice, given the strong character of this pot roast, is a Côtes-du-Roussillon, a Château de Jau, a wine which is robust, but discreet.

4. Cover the roast with the red wine and the port, then slowly bring to a boil.

Roast of Beef Round

5. Dissolve the bouillon cube in ⅔ cup/150 ml water and pour it into the pot. Cover closely and allow to cook very slowly for at least 2 hours. Check from time to time to make sure the meat is not sticking.

6. Trim the remaining vegetables, leaving the pearl onions whole. Poach each separately, without over-cooking. When the meat is done, set it aside and keep warm. Strain the cooking liquid and thicken with the potato flour dissolved in 3 tbsp water. Slice the roast, pour on the sauce and surround with the vegetables.

Veal Hock with

1. Salt and pepper the veal hock and brown it thoroughly in oil in a heavy kettle. Add the onion, chopped very finely.

Ingredients:
1 veal hock
3½ tbsp /50 ml oil
2 onions
1 glass Grand Marnier
1 tbsp flour
1 stalk celery
2 cloves garlic
1 bouquet garni
1 tomato
1 cup/250 ml dry white wine
2 oranges
salt and pepper

Serves 6
Preparation time: 15 minutes
Cooking time: 1 hour 30 minutes
Difficulty: ✳

2. Once the onions are nicely colored, flambé the meat with the Grand Marnier.

A veal hock with its beautifully rich marrow-bone is a familiar friend. Boned, it is often the base of the great classic *blanquette de veau* or a rich veal stew. Our chef has pulled out all the stops to produce a veritable concerto of flavors. This recipe works equally well with duck, or any other white meat.

To avoid lumps in the gravy, dissolve the flour well in the liquid first. Or you can use *beurre manié* (see glossary).

The Grand Marnier should be flambéed to reduce its alcohol content. This sophisticated procedure with its dancing blue flames will also liven the cuisine by providing a touch of drama and spectacle. The orange peels must be blanched two or three times to remove any bitterness. This will allow them to harmonize agreeably with the Grand Marnier, which is universally recognized as the quintessential orange liqueur.

To bring this example of classic cuisine to the apotheosis of culinary perfection, place the hock on a circle of hot saffron rice sprinkled and trimmed with chives and arrange orange sections—either fresh with membranes removed, or candied—to form a border around the radiant bed of deep yellow rice.

With its fruited overtones, this dish is perfect for an intimate dinner *tête à tête*, or with a close circle of friends.

The acidity of the Gamay grape is often paired with sweet-and-sour preparations, a tradition which leads our wine expert to suggest a Chiroubles.

3. Sprinkle the flour over the hock and onions, coating all surfaces well. Chop the celery and peel the garlic.

4. Add the celery, garlic, bouquet garni and the tomato, which has been peeled, seeded and crushed. Lightly sauté all the ingredients.

Grand Marnier

5. Add the white wine and ⅔ cup/150 ml water. Cover and allow to cook for an hour. Season with salt and pepper.

6. Carefully peel 1 orange and julienne the rind. Blanch it 2 or 3 times and add to the veal hock. Allow the flavors to blend for 10 minutes or so. Remove the veal hock to a warm platter of saffron rice surrounded by orange segments. Strain the sauce through a fine sieve, nap on the meat, and serve very hot.

Pork Jowls

1. Blanch the boned calf's foot, then cook it in the wine which has been seasoned with the bouquet garni and salt and pepper. Allow to simmer, covered, for 1 hour.

Ingredients:
2.2 lbs/1 kg pork jowls
1 calf's foot
4 cups/1 liters red wine
1 tbsp/15 ml oil
1 onion
1¼ lbs/600 g carrots
6½ tbsp/100g butter
2.2 lbs/1 kg potatoes
1 bouquet garni
1 bunch of parsley
1 bunch of chervil
salt and pepper

Serves 4
Preparation time: 25 minutes
Cooking time: 2 hours 10 minutes
Difficulty: ✷✷

2. Clean and wipe the pork jowls. In a frying pan, brown them in oil. Add salt and pepper.

Charles Monselet, poet and gastronome, sang the glory of the lowly pig: "For every part of you is generous, flesh, fat, innards." He could have added, "even your jowls." The jowls are those parts constituted by the muscles of the lower jaw. They are considered "offal," but are treated separately because they are after all muscle tissue and not innards. Don't hesitate to ask your butcher to bone the calf's foot to spare you the simple but somewhat onerous task of doing it yourself.

Allow the onions to color slightly before adding the carrots to achieve a pleasing color in the sauce. Our chef has chosen dark yellow potatoes with a firm flesh, whose texture and color will hold up well during cooking.

Be careful with the carrots because alcohol toughens them. To avoid this problem, let the rounds steam gently in their own pot until the sauce has been finished off with the butter. This approach will forestall the possibility of the vegetable toughening.

Simple, rustic and economical, this homespun recipe will easily make its way into your repertoire of family menus—but it is not at all out of place in more formal meals, either. Its congenial presence will grace any gathering of friends.

This country dish inspires roguish associations that make an earthy Beaujolais just the thing: perhaps a Morgon.

3. Peel and slice the onion; pare the carrots and cut into thin rounds. Lightly sauté the onion in oil in a heavy kettle. Augment the onions with a tablespoon of butter, and add the carrots. Cook briefly together.

4. Peel and pare the potatoes into the classic oval shape preferred by French chefs, and boil them in salted water.

with Carrots

5. Add the pork jowls to the carrots and onions. Season with salt and pepper.

6. Add the calf's foot and its juices to the pork and finish cooking. Remove the meat and vegetables, strain the sauce, and whisk in bits of butter. Mound the car-rots and onions in the center of a platter, surround with pork, and nap with hot gravy. Arrange potatoes alter-nately with meat. Garnish with parsley and chervil.

Veal Medallions

1. Peel the carrots, turnips, potatoes, and celery root. Remove the rind and membranes from the limes and separate the segments. Cut the peeled ginger into a fine julienne. Round the edges of the carrots and the turnips to make attractive shapes.

Ingredients:
1 fillet of veal
4 carrots
4 turnips
2 potatoes
1 celery root
2 limes
2¾ oz/ 80 g fresh ginger
4 tsp/20 g sugar
6½ tbsp/100g butter
1 lemon
3 tbsp flour
1 tbsp/15 ml oil
6½ tbsp/100 ml crème
    fraîche
4 tbsp soy sauce
1¼ cup/300 ml milk
salt and pepper

Serves 4
Preparation time: 30 minutes
Cooking time: 35 minutes
Difficulty: ✶

2. Add the sugar and a little butter to a pot of water, introduce the carrots and turnips, and simmer. Cut the lemon into wedges, add it to the milk, and cook the celery root and potatoes in it.

Trust this tip: Veal, ginger and lime will win you your own triple crown and bring you a windfall of success. Here are a few suggestions for the steps that follow:

Don't forget to sprinkle the juice of a lemon on the celery-root purée so it will not darken. Potatoes contain starch, and in this case the chef has included them to bind the ingredients into a smooth ensemble.

The butter added to the cooking water will lightly glaze the vegetables. The sugar used in the preparation of the turnips is meant to lessen the bitter undertone they often have. Ginger must cook for quite some time, so slice it very thin. Begin with the ginger (Step 4) and then work on the rest of the recipe.

Originating in India and Malaysia and cultivated in hot climates, the piquant flavor of ginger is an important condiment in oriental cuisine. Although it joined the western culinary tradition a long time ago, its use had been limited to candy-making. It is only fairly recently that it has been more widely used as a seasoning for meat and fish.

Ginger has better tonic effects than pepper: It distills a sweet warmth in the body and its benefits are lasting. It is a stimulant and some say it has aphrodisiac properties. Its perfume and flavor will add a touch of the exotic to your dinner parties.

This dish, so spicy and vigorous, needs a virile wine to accompany it. Our wine expert recommends a white Châteauneuf-du-Pape.

3. Cut the fillet into medallions, salt, pepper, and flour them. In a frying pan sauté the veal in small amounts of oil and butter.

4. Blanch the ginger in 2 or 3 changes of water. Cook it over low heat, incorporating half the crème fraîche and 1 tbsp sugar. Put the celery root through a food mill.

with Ginger and Lime

5. Complete the celery mousseline by blending in the rest of the crème fraîche. Salt and pepper lightly. Allow the ginger mixture to reduce, then finish it by whisking in the bits of butter, one at a time.

6. Add the soy sauce to the gravy, and stir the mixture lightly with a whisk. Serve the medallions with the sauce, and crown each portion with lime segments and a few pieces of ginger. Surround the meat with the carrots, potatoes, turnips, and the purée of celery root.

Grandmother's Pork

1. Bone the chops; set the bones aside.

Ingredients:
6 pork chops
10½ oz/300 g porcini
   mushrooms
1 egg
5¼ oz/150 g *crépine*
   (pork caul) or other
   caul
1 tbsp oil
salt and pepper

Serves 4
Preparation time: 25 minutes
Cooking time: 15 minutes
Difficulty: ✶✶

2. Chop the meat coarsely by hand or with a food processor, and place in a bowl.

Pork is the pre-eminent favorite among meats for the French, although Grimod de La Reynière claimed that pork was unsuitable for distinguished tables. But our chef entrusts us with a simple and traditional recipe which proves that excellence can in fact be earned, and that popular tastes have not only a certain honesty, but a nobility as well.

The pork chops should be cooked in two steps to bring them to perfection: They must be fried to brown them, and are then put into the oven to finish cooking.

If you opt for an accompaniment of potato gratin, the heat of the oven can bake the chops at the same time as it cooks the potatoes. As a variation, replace the wild mushrooms by asparagus points and the pork by the same cut of veal.

Don't save this delectable dish just for your family. Invite your friends. They will appreciate the simple pleasure you offer them with this recipe.

It is always good to discover for yourself or to introduce to others an obscure wine which is at once cheerful and appetizing! Our wine expert suggests a red Gaillac.

3. Chop the porcini and incorporate them along with the egg into the chopped meat.

4. Season the stuffing with salt and pepper, mixing the ingredients together thoroughly. Spread open a crépine and place a bone and about 3 tablespoons of the stuffing on the caul.

Chops en Crépine

5. Wrap the crépine around the stuffing and form it into the shape of a pork chop.

6. Heat the oil in a frying pan. Salt and pepper the stuffed "chops" and brown them evenly. Place them in an uncovered oven-proof dish, and bake for about 30 minutes in a medium oven. Serve the chops en crépine with a tomato sauce.

Fillet of Lamb with

1. Bone the saddle of lamb. In a heavy pot, brown the bones well in some olive oil. Add the chopped carrot, onions, garlic and rosemary. Salt and pepper the vegetables, and cook briefly. Add water to cover and allow the lamb broth to simmer.

Ingredients:
1 saddle of lamb
2 tbsp olive oil
1 carrot
2 onions
1 clove garlic
1 sprig rosemary
1 generous lb/500 g
    white beans (coco)
2 stalks of Swiss
    chard
2 tbsp crème fraîche
1 tbsp parmesan
    cheese
6 black olives
2 tomatoes
½ cup/120 g butter
½ sprig basil
salt and pepper

Serves 6
Preparation time: 35 minutes
Cooking time: 30 minutes
Difficulty: ✲✲

You will note the pleasure our chef takes in composing a dish graphically, as though making a sketch or even a good-humored caricature. And the bundles he creates have pleasant surprises in store since they contain a common vegetable whose charms we often overlook. Swiss chard is found in many kitchen gardens. But for this treatment you must keep your eye on the stove throughout the various procedures.

Blanch the Swiss chard fronds briefly in salted water so they will be easier to handle when making the bundles. In the second step, the white stalks require longer cooking than the green leaves.

What makes this recipe so attractive is that one may prepare the vegetables the night before. The same is true of the lamb broth. Only the meat must be cooked the day of the meal. The other elements can easily be reheated.

Also, the white beans may be replaced by fava or lima beans, which would add a lively green note to the preparation.

If the dish cools down before you have brought all its elements together, reheat the lamb briefly in a warm oven: This will result in a succulent meal which will delight the palate. It would be perfect for a congenial Sunday dinner with friends and family.

The suggested wine is a Madiran: Château de Montus, an aristocratic wine hearty and yet full of subtleties.

2. Place the pre-soaked beans in a heavy pot, and boil them in water. Add salt ¾ of the way through the cooking.

3. Wash the Swiss chard thoroughly. Remove the green leaves from the stocks, blanch them briefly, and set aside. Cut the white stalks into small dice.

4. Poach the diced white stalks of the chard until ¾ cooked. Drain them, add the crème fraîche and parmesan cheese, and finish cooking. When cool, place a spoonful of diced stalks on each of the 4 Swiss chard leaves, and fold the sides to make packages.

Swiss Chard Bundles

5. Pit and mince the olives. Peel, seed and dice the tomatoes. Cut the basil into fine strips. Drain the cooked beans, then add half the tomatoes and the basil. Moisten the beans with gravy made by whisking butter into a little lamb broth. Let simmer.

6. Strain and reduce the remaining gravy. Halve the lamb fillet and sauté in a frying pan with a little olive oil. Season with salt and pepper. Slice the meat and arrange it on a serving platter. Moisten with the hot lamb broth, and decorate the plate with the Swiss chard bundles, tomatoes, olives, and beans.

Poultry in Parchment

1. Peel and finely chop the shallots, and brown them in 1 tsp butter. Add the port and the cognac, and reduce by half. Incorporate the beef stock, salt lightly, add pepper, and cook for about 15 minutes. Strain this sauce through a fine sieve and set aside.

2. Clean the chicken breasts. Season with salt and pepper. Wrap them in the cauls. Fry the foie gras slices lightly in an anti-stick pan and set aside.

Ingredients:

4 5¼-oz/150-g chicken breasts, boned and skinned
12 oz/350 g *crépine* or other caul
12 thin slices of foie gras of duck
2 shallots
3½ tbsp/50 g butter
⅔ cup/150 ml port or Madeira
3½ tbsp/50 ml cognac
1¼ cup/300 ml beef broth (see basic recipe)
2 tbsp oil
1½ oz/40g truffles
1 tbsp potato starch
salt and pepper
parchment

Serves 4
Preparation time: 35 minutes
Cooking time: 35 minutes
Difficulty: ✶✶

Sauce périgueux is one of the most prestigious classics of French cuisine. It is made by reducing Madeira, or port, and truffle juice, and is often enhanced by thin slices of truffles. The Périgord noir has long been the province of France which boasts the very best varieties of truffles. This elite class of mushrooms is known locally as "black diamonds." It is doubtless for this reason that the sauce, with its rich gastronomic lineage, has been named after the capital of this province in southwestern France, a veritable pilgrim's goal for serious gourmets.

En papillotes is a sophisticated form of cooking which requires great precision and a certain dexterity in the folding of the parchment paper which envelopes the preparation. This pleated package will hold the mixture carefully enclosed as it swells during cooking. The *crépine* will keep the poultry breasts from drying out, and the aroma which wafts from the package as it is opened will be sublime.

Any poultry is adaptable to this recipe. Small veal medallions would work admirably, if that is your whim.

With their mild but pronounced aromas, these *papillotes* are true jewels that you will be proud to serve to your very best friends.

Our wine expert suggest a Gevrey-Chambertin—a really peerless Burgundy. Drink it and discover the dark cherry overtones which make it such a superb choice for this dish.

3. Sauté the wrapped breasts in a frying pan with the oil over low heat. Add the chopped truffles and allow to simmer.

4. Mix the potato starch with water to form a paste and use it to bind the sauce from Step 1. Adjust the seasoning, heat well, and whisk in the remaining butter, a bit at a time. Remove the breasts from the crépine and scallop the meat.

with Périgueux Sauce

5. Fold a parchment sheet in two. Using scissors, cut out a half circle. Unfold the paper and place 2 chicken breasts and 3 small slices of foie gras on it. Add a small spoonful of the Périgueux sauce.

6. Seal the edge airtight, following the perimeter of the circle. Repeat the process with the other 2 breasts. Place the papillotes on a cookie sheet or in a shallow pan and bake for 5 or 6 minutes. Serve with the vegetables of your choice.

Pauillac Lamb

1. Blanch the sweetbread, placing it in cold water and then heating the water. Remove and refresh it under cold water, drain, and set aside.

Ingredients:
2 fillets of lamb
1 lamb sweetbread
1 onion
1 carrot
2 cloves garlic
6½ tbsp/100 ml oil
⅔ cup/150 ml white wine
¾ cup/200 g butter
2 truffles
9 oz/250 g lentins or other mushrooms
1 bunch of chives
salt and pepper

Serves 4
Preparation time: 20 minutes
Cooking time: 30 minutes
Difficulty: ✷

2. Peel the onion and carrot and dice them. Peel the garlic cloves, cut them in half, and remove the germ.

Pauillac lamb is raised in an area which boasts what are indisputably the finest wines of France. Its quality is so exceptional that it ranks as highly among meats as its analogue, the great red wine of the Haut-Médoc. The climate and the nature of the soil of this lovely corner of France are the main factors in the excellence of its lamb. Our chef has, quite naturally, inherited some of the same high standards that are part of his birthright.

The lentin is a mushroom of Chinese origin which, while not widespread, can now be found in France. It grows on oak logs in the Périgord. If they are unavailable, substitute *pleurotes*, or oyster mushrooms, which are available year round in oriental markets.

If truffles are a luxury to grace only exceptional occasions, they can be replaced by morels or *trompettes de la mort* (literally "trumpets of death"). These, too, give off the delicious perfume of the forest.

Be very scrupulous when cooking the lamb. It must be golden brown outside, but remain pink the inside. Allow the meat to gather its juices before serving. It will be all the more tender and succulent for the pause, but serve it while still hot. This Pauillac lamb with truffles should not be reheated. And you can be sure it won't be necessary, for this dish is so refined that gourmets will pitch in and finish every last mouthful.

Since this meal provides a joyous occasion, our wine expert suggests you empty your piggy bank and serve the only wine in the world known to have made an interplanetary voyage: the Lynch-Bages.

3. In a heavy pot, sauté the onion and carrot in a little oil. Add the garlic and sweetbread, and allow them to color up. Remove the sweetbread and deglaze the pan with the white wine. Replace the sweetbread, season the pan with salt and pepper, cover, and cook until done.

4. In a frying pan, salt and pepper the lamb fillets and fry them in oil and some of the butter.

with Truffles

5. In another frying pan brown the mushrooms in a little butter and then season them.

6. Remove the fillets and deglaze the pan with juice from the sweetbreads and mushrooms. Reduce, strain, and finish the sauce by whisking in bits of butter. Peel and cube the sweetbread and place it on a platter. Arrange the thinly scalloped lamb fillets around the edge. Nap with the sauce and garnish with chives.

Breast of Duck with

Ingredients:
2 duck breasts
12 oz/350 g carrots
10½ oz/300 g turnips
10 tbsp/150 g butter
1 tbsp sugar
5¼ oz/150 g foie gras
   of duck
1 oz/30 g truffles
½ glass white wine
salt and pepper

Serves 4
Preparation time: 30 minutes
Cooking time: 15 minutes
Difficulty: ✶✶

1. Remove excess fat from the duck breasts, then salt and pepper them. Peel the carrots and turnips and cut them into coarse julienne.

2. Add a little butter and a tablespoon of sugar to just enough salted water to cover the vegetables and cook briefly, leaving them somewhat crisp and fresh in color.

Here we have a delectable bouquet that brings together the three signature products of the Périgord: duck breast, foie gras, and truffles. These ingredients are the pride of this heartland of French gastronomy. Rich in tastes and aromas, these luxurious elements join to make an unusually rich and harmonious culinary delight.

If you wish to caramelize the vegetables, sprinkle them with water and add a spoonful each of butter and sugar. Cook over low heat until the water evaporates. The glaze that remains will make them slightly sweet and brilliant in color. To keep them fresh and crisp, be careful not to cook them too long.

The carrots or turnips could be replaced by small potatoes. The duck can also be accompanied by a compote of garlic, prepared by heating peeled garlic cloves with a little butter and two tablespoons of sugar. Cover with water and, using aluminum foil as a lid, cook slowly until the liquid evaporates. Let the garlic color up lightly. This is also a real treat.

Sear the breasts on the skin side in a pan without oil, but remember the duck should be served very rare. This dish is meant to be eaten hot, as soon as it is cooked; it is a party in and of itself. Colorful and delicious, it is sure to delight both the eye and the palate.

Our wine expert suggests that the attractive bouquet of a great Saint-Émilion, such as the Château Patris, will be a very pleasant complement to the succulent preparation of the duck breasts.

3. In a hot pan, sauté the breasts skin side down, taking care to keep them on the rare side.

4. Cut the foie gras into slivers and set aside. When the breasts are cooked, remove them from the pan and pour off ¾ of the fat.

Fois Gras and Truffles

5. Add the white wine to the pan, reduce for 2 minutes, then add the foie gras. Simmer several minutes.

6. Add the truffles and allow them to simmer for 30 seconds. Cut the breast into thin slices and arrange on a platter with the foie gras. Nap on the sauce and serve very hot with the caramelized vegetables.

1. Carefully remove the excess fat from the duck breasts. Season with salt and pepper, and dredge lightly with the flour.

Ingredients:
2 duck breasts
6½ tbsp/50 g flour
3½ tbsp/50 g butter
1 generous lb/500 g cooked foie gras of duck
1 generous lb/500 g puff pastry (see basic recipe)
1 egg
1 cup/250 ml Madeira sauce (see basic recipe)
salt and pepper

Serves 4
Preparation time: 40 minutes
Cooking time: 20 minutes
Difficulty: ✳✳

2. In a frying pan, sauté the breasts gently in butter, being careful to keep them rare. Set them aside and let cool.

This recipe was christened "Cardinal's Slippers" in honor of an early Bishop of Luçon—the town after which our chef's restaurant is named. The cleric possessed the reputation of both having a solid appetite and preferring food of high quality. It seems that as soon as he arrived at a stagecoach stop, he would take off his shoes and put on his slippers, doubtless better to prepare himself for the delights of a fine dinner. Be it legend or truth, the story demonstrates how earthly delights can be enjoyed while awaiting more ethereal pleasures to come.

This recipe is a true voyage to the heart of the Landais, renowned for its outstanding poultry. So well-balanced are the delicacies of the palate in this recipe, that it is hard to say whether the flavor of the breast brings out the foie gras, or the other way around.

Our chef cannot resist the enchanting attraction of truffles, but "trumpets of the dead" (*trompettes de la mort*) or black chanterelles both go very well with the Madeira sauce. Sautéed potatoes make good companions for the mushrooms.

The chef emphasizes the importance of the cooking time: 10 minutes in a very hot oven. This is therefore a dish that can be prepared at the last minute. For a festive meal, this wonderful alliance of fine ingredients will be sure to please every appetite.

The richness of the mushrooms, the duck breast, and the foie gras dictates an unctuous Saint-Émilion: a Château Figeac.

3. Slice the foie gras thinly, and set aside. Prepare the pastry according to the basic recipe and roll it out into a thin square sheet.

4. After the breasts have cooled, cut them into thin slices. Lay the sliced duck and foie gras on the pastry square in alternating layers.

Slippers

5. Roll the pastry around the sliced meat into a kind of giant turnover, giving it the form of a slipper.

6. Pinch the edges of the pastry lightly to seal, brush the surface with the beaten egg, and bake in a very hot oven for 8 to 10 minutes. Serve your pastry slippers very hot alongside the mushrooms and sautéed potatoes, topping the vegetables with the Madeira sauce.

Chicken à la

1. Cut the chicken into 4 pieces and bone them.
Sprinkle with salt and pepper, dredge with the flour, and
brown them in some of the butter in an ovenproof dish.

Ingredients:
1 2½-lb/1.2-kg free-range,
   corn-fed chicken
1 tbsp flour
¼ cup/60 g butter
1 glass dry white wine
   (preferably a Tursan)
2 beef bouillon cubes or
   2 glasses of stock (see
   basic recipe)
1 tbsp/15 g *beurre manié*
   (see glossary)
2 thick slices Bayonne
   (dry-cured) ham
7 oz/200 g cèpes or
   mushrooms
Armagnac
2 tbsp pine nuts
salt and pepper

Serves 4
Preparation time: 40 minutes
Cooking time: 30 minutes
Difficulty: ✷

2. Bake the fowl in the oven until tender. Degrease the
pan and pour in the white wine.

This recipe was created 20 years ago by the father of our chef, on the occasion of a dinner
in the Eiffel Tower restaurant planned as a showcase of regional products.

La Goudalière is an association of connoisseurs who celebrate the gastronomic riches of
the Landes. Our recipe calls for products from the region's fields, farms, and pine forests:
the cured ham of Bayonne, wild mushrooms, and notably, the succulent chicken bearing
its famous red label certifying it as being free-range and fattened on corn.

A sauce is always best reduced at medium heat: Let the liquid simmer while stirring with
a wooden spoon until the liquid thickens. This also eliminates the wine's acidity.

If you use pre-cooked bouillon or gravy, improve the flavor by simmering onions and
carrots in it. Add a touch of Armagnac to the sauce just before serving, and for a final
flourish, toss in some toasted pine nuts.

This chicken dish is easy to prepare and takes well to reheating.

You can add further delight to this voyage of the palate by choosing a delicious
traditional accompaniment: corn cakes.

For the majority of the French, chicken has become the most popular meat. This
preparation will take it from the banal and restore some of its character and originality.
Our wine expert proposes a Madiran, but since the younger varieties can be a bit rough,
she suggests you choose a vintage at least five years old.

3. Allow the wine to reduce until almost dry, then
dissolve the bouillon cubes in 2 glasses of water and
add, or use the same amount of prepared beef stock.

4. Adjust the seasoning of the sauce if necessary, then
incorporate the beurre manié into it.

Goudalière

5. Dice the ham. In separate frying pans, brown the pieces of ham and the mushrooms in butter.

6. Strain the sauce through a fine sieve. Add to it the ham, the mushrooms and a splash of Armagnac, and let it boil briefly. Nap the sauce over the chicken, sprinkle with lightly roasted pine nuts, and serve very hot along with corn cakes.

Veal Chops

1. Salt and pepper the chops lightly and flour them. Cut the peppers into large quarters.

Ingredients:
4 veal chops
flour for dredging
2 red peppers
3½ tbsp/50 ml oil
3½ tbsp /50 g butter
2 thick slices Bayonne (dry-cured) ham
½ glass white wine
6½ tbsp/100 ml crème fraîche
1 cube beef bouillon
1 tbsp/15 g *beurre manié*
3½ tbsp/50 ml Madeira
salt and pepper

Serves 4
Preparation time: 15 minutes
Cooking time: 20 minutes
Difficulty: ✰

2. In a frying pan, slowly sauté the chops in the oil and butter.

Only milk-fed veal is of choice quality. Certain country butchers actually refer to it as being still "within its mother." Such meat will assuredly be first rate—very pale, with satiny white fat. Milk-fed veal is tender, delicate, and highly prized in good cuisine.

Avoid over-cooking the Bayonne ham, as it tends to become excessively salty. A quick turn in the frying pan is all that is needed.

You can also apply this method of preparation to pork chops, being careful to maintain the mellow succulence of the meat. For variety, the vegetable garnish can be altered according to your tastes.

These chops will bring a warm and congenial note of color and harmony to a family meal. Serve the platter hot and enjoy this dish! It can be reheated, but the flavor will be best when it is served straight out of the oven.

Our wine expert, wishing to bring out the succulence of the veal and its tenderness, chooses a fruity Savigny-lès-Beaune.

3. Set the veal aside in a warm dish. Briefly sauté the peppers together with the ham.

4. On a platter, arrange the pepper pieces and ham on top of the chops. Pour the excess grease out of the pan, deglaze it with the wine, and reduce the liquid for 2 minutes.

à la Chef

5. Add the crème fraîche to the pan, and carefully stir the mixture to blend well. Allow it to simmer over low heat for a few minutes.

6. Add the bouillon cube dissolved in a glass of water, or a glass of meat stock, to the pan. Slowly introduce bits of beurre manié into the sauce. Stir in the Madeira. Allow to simmer for several minutes. Adjust the seasoning, and nap the veal chops with the sauce. Serve with a risotto.

Spring Chicken

Ingredients:
3 spring chickens
3½ tbsp/50 g butter
2 cups/500 ml crème
  fraîche
3 tbsp port
1 shallot
7 tbsp hazelnut purée
6 oz/175 g whole
  hazelnuts (filberts)
salt and pepper

1. Clean the chickens well, singe them, remove the wing tips, and truss the birds. Sprinkle them with salt and pepper, butter the skin, and roast in a very hot oven.

Serves 3
Preparation time: 25 minutes
Cooking time: 30 minutes
Difficulty: ✶

2. Pour the crème fraîche and the port into a casserole, and bring to a boil.

In culinary terms, a spring chicken is one that weighs about 11 ounces and whose flesh is delicately flavorful. Obviously, this represents the most tender of fowl.

Dried hazelnuts are used in the preparation of this dish. Try to buy them with their husks intact and select those whose skin is bright, smooth and unblemished. In season, of course fresh nuts are best; they add a refined succulence to the finished dish. Hazelnuts are very nourishing and rich in proteins. In addition they provide sulfur, phosphorus, calcium, and vitamins.

This recipe is not difficult to carry out. Singe the birds well before cooking to remove any stray down fibers or pin feathers.

After cooking, the bones will be able to be removed easily, and, with a little care and dexterity, the tender flesh will remain intact and unmarred.

Sautéed young small potatoes or green peas offer a harmonious accompaniment to this gourmet recipe.

If you want to push refinement to its extreme, a crisp salad dressed with hazelnut-oil and sprinkled with cracked nuts will provide a princely garnish.

Our wine expert advises a Volnay: The fruitiness of the wine will quite admirably set off the tenderness of the spring chicken.

3. Chop the shallot finely and introduce it to the crème fraîche and port mixture.

4. Stir in the hazelnut purée, whisk, and allow to reduce slowly for 10 to 12 minutes.

with Hazelnuts

5. At the end of the cooking, add salt, pepper lightly, and finish the sauce by whisking in bits of butter, one at a time.

6. Cut each chicken lengthwise into 2 pieces, splitting the breast bone. Remove the bones, place the pieces on a serving platter, and nap them with the sauce. Sprinkle with cracked nuts and serve.

Chicken Steamed

1. Cut the chicken into 4 pieces. Peel all the vegetables.

Ingredients:
1 3½-lb/1.6-kg free-range, corn-fed chicken
6½ tbsp/100 g butter
4 small leeks
1 bunch of carrots
1 bunch of turnips
1 small bundle of asparagus
1 zucchini squash
2 cups/500 ml crème fraîche
4 potatoes
a few sprigs of tarragon
salt and pepper

Serves 4
Preparation time: 1 hour
Cooking time: 40 minutes
Difficulty: ✳ ✳

2. In a heavy pan containing a spoonful of the butter, brown the fowl until golden. Sprinkle with salt and pepper.

For a member of the chicken family, to hail from the famed district of Bresse in the French province of Burgundy is to be born the best of the best. Not being from Bresse automatically excludes a bird from the aristocracy of poultry, who luxuriate in château life pampered by a diet of pure corn. It is not surprising that the flesh of such a chicken, when cooked, will attain perfection. If you cannot find a specimen from Bresse, you can settle for one from the Landais, or a well-recommended free-range fowl raised on a farm. Though these lack noble lineage, they will be succulent when prepared in this way.

This recipe can be easily accomplished by anyone willing to follow the directions faithfully: Be sure to brown the quarters of fowl on all sides. Monitor the point at which the cream in the sauce has been properly reduced by testing how it flows from a spoon. Be careful not to overwhelm the meat with a sauce that is too heavy. The reduced cream finished off with fresh chervil is simply sublime.

The originality of this recipe lies in the way it can respond to personal taste or to dictates of the season in your choice of vegetables. Keep in mind that carrots with their vitamin A are precious allies of growth and health. This fact should be uppermost when considering the children at our table.

Our wine expert suggests that for this marriage of the heart and the mind, there can be nothing better than a great Beaujolais such as a Moulin-à-Vent.

3. Cut the vegetables into roughly ovoid, cylindrical shapes with beveled edges in the French style.

4. When the chicken is golden, remove it to a 3-tiered steamer for 30 minutes. Pour off the fat from the frying pan, and deglaze the pan with a small glass of water. Stir in the crème fraîche and allow the sauce to thicken.

with Vegetables

5. After 15 minutes, at the halfway-point in the steaming of the chicken, place the vegetables in the upper tier of the steamer above the chicken. Salt the vegetables lightly, cover, and continue to cook for 15 minutes.

6. Strain the sauce, heat it, remove from the stovetop, and finish it off by whisking in bits of butter Adjust the seasoning. Place the chicken on a platter, nap it with sauce, and garnish with the vegetables and tarragon leaves.

Fillet of Veal with

1. With a sharp knife, trim the fillet, removing the nerve, and slice it into medallions.

Ingredients:
1¾ lbs/800 g prime
    fillet of veal
4 zucchini squash
2 thin carrots
1 cucumber
3½ tbsp/50 g butter
2 tbsp oil
1 chicken bouillon
    cube
6½ tbsp/100 ml port
salt and pepper

Serves 4
Preparation time: 30 minutes
Cooking time: 20 minutes
Difficulty: ✷

2. Cut the zucchini in half lengthwise and then again crosswise into 2-inch lengths. Slice the carrots into little discs. Cook the vegetables in a steamer. Season with salt and pepper.

The tenderness of a filet mignon of veal, so well reflected in its charming name, never fails to please. But a sweetbread, a good fowl, a turkey scallop, a saddle of rabbit—all these delicate meats would be well-served by this recipe.

Let the water from the zucchini evaporate by removing the cover from the steamer for a few minutes. Return the cucumber to the steamer for two minutes just before serving.

The carrots in this dish serve mainly a decorative purpose, rather than adding much taste. Be sure to degrease the pan used to cook the meat, that is to discard the excess fat, before preparing the sauce. Your sauce will be all the lighter for it, and yet retain the depth of its flavor. Adjust the seasoning if necessary: The palate is to the cook what the compass is to the lonely sailor. Our chef recommends using fresh cracked pepper because of its superior flavor.

This veal mignon must be served piping hot, with no delay. The vegetables can be reheated, but not the sauce.

What a pretty dish, light, but vitamin-rich, ideal for a lover's meal.

Veal has an affinity for white wines: Our wine expert suggests a Chablis.

3. Pass the zucchini through a food mill to obtain a coarse purée. Salt lightly.

4. Peel the cucumbers, cut them lengthwise, and remove the seeds. Slice them into a coarse julienne.

Cucumber and Zucchini

5. Bring a pot of salted water to a boil and poach the cucumber julienne lightly. Dissolve the bouillon cube in a glass of water.

6. Salt and pepper the medallions and sauté in some of the butter and oil. Remove to a warm platter. Deglaze the pan with the port, reduce, and stir in the bouillon. Arrange the vegetables around the meat. Whisk the remaining butter into the sauce bit by bit, nap the medallions with it, and serve.

Veal Tournedos

1. Remove the nerves from the veal fillet; slice it into finger-thick medallions. Peel and dice the vegetables.

Ingredients:
1 veal fillet
1 celery stalk
1 onion
2 carrots
4 mushrooms caps
6½ tbsp/100 g butter
6½ tbsp/100 ml
 Madeira
1 cup/250 ml crème
 fraîche
gnocchis (see basic
 recipe)
1 sprig of thyme
1 bunch of chives
salt and pepper

Serves 4
Preparation time: 40 minutes
Cooking time: 25 minutes
Difficulty: ✷✷

2. In a pan containing some of the butter, sauté the carrots, celery, onion, and mushroom caps in succession, leaving the mushrooms for last. Toss the vegetables lightly together and allow to cool. Season with salt and pepper, and strew with thyme.

The origin of the word tournedos may be unclear, but this gastronomic delight has nonetheless become a staple of fine cuisine. Though tournedos usually refers to medallions of beef tenderloin, in this case our chef has chosen fillet of veal. Choose the lower part of the fillet, then slice it into tournedos. Flatten the rounds by pounding them lightly so they do not shrink during cooking.

Monitor the cooking time of each vegetable, then let them return to room temperature, for the stuffing must be cold to prevent the meat from spoiling. For a real feast try foie gras in the stuffing; you will be delighted.

There are different styles of gnocchi: Parisian, Alsatian, Piemontese…. Our chef has opted to serve this dish with the Roman style. Gnocchi provide a splash of sunshine on the platter, and allow infinite variations of accompaniments: various cooked vegetables, chosen for their colors, a variety of cheeses, herbs, and condiments, all of which harmonize deliciously. Be guided by your imagination and curiosity in trying these exquisite combinations.

Although simple, this recipe for veal tournedos is in the grand tradition of French cuisine and is worthy of being the centerpiece of an important celebration.

The tenderness of the veal deserves a wine which is fruited and delicate. Our wine expert suggests a Côte-de-Beaune or a Chianti.

3. Slit the medallions without cutting all the way through. Stuff with a spoonful of the cooled vegetable mixture, and pinch the edges well.

4. Salt and pepper the stuffed tournedos, and sauté them in a pan with the rest of the butter. Be careful to keep them rare.

Stuffed with Vegetables

5. Once the medallions are done, remove from the heat and pour the fat from the pan. Add the Madeira, and let the sauce reduce by half.

6. Incorporate the crème fraîche, stirring briskly. Allow the sauce to thicken. Season with salt and pepper. Strain the sauce, then add the minced chives. Place the veal on a platter surrounded by crescents of grilled gnocchi, and nap with the sauce.

Christmas Turkey

1. Peel and dice the mushrooms and apples. Sauté in oil in separate pans. In a heavy pot, brown the chopped shallots in butter. Add the port and white wine to the shallots, and allow to reduce by half.

2. Clean the chicken livers and sear them in oil. Add salt and pepper. Cook for 2 minutes, then drain them and chop into small pieces.

Ingredients:
1 turkey
For the stuffing:
7 oz/200 g mushrooms
3 apples; 10 shallots
6½ tbsp/100 ml oil
3½ tbsp/50g butter
3½ tbsp/50 ml port
6½ tbsp/100 ml white wine
7 oz/200 g chicken liver
28 oz/800 g chestnuts
¾ cup/200 ml milk
2 egg yolks
6½ tbsp/100g crème fraîche
nutmeg; cayenne pepper
For the pan gravy:
2 onions; 1 carrot; 1 leek
2 stalks celery
¾ cup/200 ml veal stock
salt and pepper

Serves 8
Preparation time: 45 minutes
Cooking time: 2 hours
Difficulty: ✫✫

For many people, a Christmas dinner without turkey and chestnut stuffing is a bit like Santa Claus with an empty bag. On this exceptional day, a little extra time in the kitchen is justified. In fact, the preparations actually increase the pleasure because you know your efforts will add substantially to the joy of all who gather at your table.

Care taken with the numerous details of the recipe will repay your efforts richly, beginning with the ingredients for the stuffing, which must all be cut into fine dice.

The milk added to the cooking water of the chestnuts sweetens them and maintains their color. The celery adds a delicious touch of flavor.

Baste the turkey often as it cooks so that it stays moist and tender. After the first hour and a half of baking, cover it with aluminum foil. The steam which condenses on the foil will fall back into the roasting pan and contribute to the succulence of the turkey.

To prevent the juices from caramelizing too quickly, begin baking the turkey in a slow oven and raise the temperature gradually. Also, as for all roasted meats, let the turkey rest in a warm spot (perhaps in the open oven or on its door) at least fifteen minutes before carving to gather its juices. Its flavor will be wonderful!

This is a holiday! Go to the cellar and bring up your best bottles of Savigny-lès-Beaune.

3. Peel the chestnuts and poach them in milk and salted water. Add the mushrooms and apples to the reduced shallot mixture.

4. Incorporate the liver and drained chestnuts into the stuffing mixture. Salt and pepper. Add a bit of grated nutmeg and cayenne and combine everything thoroughly.

with Chestnut Stuffing

5. Blend the egg yolks and crème fraîche into the stuffing mixture, and mix well. Peel the onions and carrot to be used for the gravy. Clean the leek and the celery; chop all these vegetables coarsely. Clean the turkey and spoon stuffing loosely into its cavity.

6. Truss the bird securely. Rub the skin with oil and butter; salt and pepper. Put the vegetables in the roasting pan with the turkey. Roast in a medium oven for 1½ hours. After 45 min, add the stock to deglaze the pan. Baste occasionally. Just before serving, strain the pan juices; serve as sauce with the carved turkey.

Chicken Stewed

1. Clean, singe and truss the chicken. Peel and chop the onions and carrot. Separate the garlic heads.

Ingredients:
- 1 3½-lb/1.5-kg stewing chicken
- 2 onions
- 1 carrot
- 2 large heads of garlic
- 1 handful wood avens, bennet
- 4 cups/1 liter chicken stock
- 2 cups/500 ml crème fraîche
- 6½ tbsp/100 g butter
- 1 bouquet garni
- salt and pepper

Serves 6
Preparation time: 15 minutes
Cooking time: 1 hour 30 minutes
Difficulty: ✶

2. In a heavy pan containing a little butter, brown the onions and carrot with the bouquet garni.

Yes, it is true! This stew, originally a rustic country recipe, is made with the perfumed grasses found on hillsides or at the edges of fields. The scented bouquet is made of all sorts of spring greens (wood avens or herb bennet), and other tiny flowered wild plants gathered in June, and air-dried through summer to be at their best by October.

In this manner you can cook veal, pork, or perch that you might be lucky enough to catch yourself. In certain mountain areas, ham is dried in a bundle of these grasses and is said to be very succulent. These greens risk being a bit dusty so wash them in copious running water before using The beneficent rinsing will only add to the cachet of the dish.

Use a reasonable amount of grass; a handful is enough. Too much grass will leave a bitter after-taste. If you prefer a strong taste, add a dozen heads of unpeeled garlic to further enrich the country flavor.

To assure the proper cooking of the fowl, test it with a knitting needle from inside the cavity so as to leave the skin intact. The liquid will run clear when the chicken is done, but a pink color means that at least 20 more minutes will be required.

This original preparation is virtually unknown in the city, but is loved in the countryside. With its startling aromas it will thrill any gourmet, and particularly delight those gastronomes who like to keep noble culinary traditions alive.

Our wine expert suggests a white Saint-Joseph, an original wine with honeyed overtones.

3. Salt and pepper the chicken. Wash the dried grass generously in running water.

4. Place the chicken in the pot on top of the vegetables.

in Sweet Grasses

5. Surround the chicken with the grasses together with the cloves of garlic. Add the chicken stock, and bake in the oven for a good hour.

6. Remove the chicken from the oven and lay on a decorative bed of grass on a serving platter. Strain the cooking liquids, reduce gently, add the crème fraîche, and allow the sauce to thicken. Adjust the seasoning. Finish the sauce by whisking in bits of butter. Serve with the chicken surrounded by unpeeled garlic cloves.

Chicken

1. Clean the chicken, truss it with string, and season with salt and pepper. Roast in a heavy kettle until ¾ done, then set aside. Peel and finely chop the shallots. Peel the pearl onions. Brown the onions and shallots in a little butter over low heat.

2. Peel and gut the eel. Cut into 1¼-in/3 cm slices. Sear them in a frying pan in a little oil. Sprinkle with salt and pepper.

Ingredients:
1 3¼-lb/1.5-kg chicken
2.2 lbs/1 kg eels
4 shallots
6½ tbsp/100g butter
6½ tbsp/100 ml cooking oil
8¾ oz/250 g mushrooms
5¾ oz/150 g pearl onions
2 cups/500 ml white wine
2 cups/500 ml crème fraîche
½ bunch of chives
salt and pepper

Serves 8
Preparation time: 30 minutes
Cooking time: 1 hour 30 minutes
Difficulty: ✳✳

Eels and chicken—the combination is surprising indeed. You will doubtless be the first among your circle of friends to present this original recipe! Traditionally served in bistros near the city gates of canal and river towns in France, this dish is today a rare (but much appreciated) classic. A variation is to substitute a lamprey for the classic eel.

Since the blood of eels is bitter, the pieces of eel must be soaked and rinsed in cold running water to eliminate the pronounced taste. To lighten the dish, it is important to degrease the broth. Let it sit until the fat rises to the surface; then it can be easily removed with a ladle or skimming spoon.

Although not very difficult, the recipe does take quite a bit of time. Plan two good hours of work, including the cooking time. If you wish to interrupt the preparation, stop just before the crème fraîche is added to the sauce. Then reheat the food slowly, and add the crème fraîche just before serving.

Otherwise, incorporate the cream directly after skimming the kettle. If you want to further thicken the sauce, a spoonful of corn starch dissolved in water will do the trick. This chicken dish is unique. Reserve it for a special Sunday for curious friends who are connoisseurs willing to try something different.

Our wine expert suggests a Sylvaner.

3. Add the eel pieces to the onions and shallots and cook over low heat.

4. Incorporate the mushrooms into the mixture, and stir in the white wine.

with Eels

5. Add the chicken to the kettle, cover, and simmer for about 15 minutes. Remove the chicken and set it aside. Stir the crème fraîche into the sauce and mix delicately. Allow the sauce to simmer and thicken. Adjust the seasoning. Let it reduce by half.

6. Place the chicken on a serving platter, surrounded by mushrooms, onions and pieces of eel. Sprinkle with chipped chives. Strain the sauce, remove it from the heat and enrich by whirling in the rest of the butter in bits. Serve alongside the platter.

Rabbit Roulades

1. Soak the flageolet beans in cold water overnight, then drain them and cook in water with the bouquet garni, 1 carrot, and 1 onion studded with whole cloves. Allow to simmer. At the end of the cooking, salt and pepper lightly.

Ingredients:
2 saddles of rabbit
2 rabbit livers
7 oz/200 g flageolets
2 carrots
2 onions
6½ tbsp/100 ml peanut oil
2 cloves garlic
6½ tbsp/100 ml white wine
10½ oz/300 g chanterelles
1 tbsp olive oil
3½ tbsp/50 ml vinegar
6½ tbsp/100 g butter
1 bouquet garni
cloves, rosemary, thyme
bay leaf
1 sprig of basil
3 sprigs of Italian parsley
salt and pepper

Serves 4
Preparation time: 1 hour 45 minutes
Cooking time: 1 hour 30 minutes
Difficulty: ✶✶✶

2. Season the rabbit livers with salt, pepper, and rosemary, and sauté lightly in a pan containing 1 tbsp of peanut oil.

Colorful and picturesque, this recipe is a treasury of flavors and aromas that will perfume the house well before meal-time, making mouths water in anticipation.

You probably have met field salad—also known as purslane, corn salad or lamb's lettuce—with its wide leaves, or a cultivated variety of *claytone de Cuba* which, despite its name, is grown in France and Belgium. Rich in magnesium, this kitchen garden plant is slightly piquant, and can either be eaten as a salad or, provided the stems and leaves are still young, prepared like spinach.

The rabbit in this recipe can be replaced by poultry breasts or veal liver. Parents concerned with proper nutrition for their children might well choose veal liver because of its high vitamin D content.

Our chef advises, in initially sautéing the rabbit livers for this recipe, not to let them go beyond the rare stage, since they will continue to cook along with the rabbit.

Let the sauce reduce slowly, so it will absorb the whole gamut of flavors.

This dish is meant to be eaten hot, but in summer you may well also appreciate it cold. This delicate *plat de résistance* will delight your guests. They will surely recognize its wonderful originality.

Our wine expert's choice is a dry Vouvray; the unmistakable flavor of the Chenin grape from which this wine is made will make a joyful companion to this unique dish.

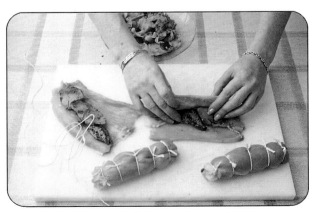

3. Bone the saddles of rabbit, and cut them in two. Salt and pepper their inner surfaces, roll them around the partially cooked livers, and tie securely.

4. Brown the roulades lightly in olive oil. Chop the remaining carrot and onion coarsely. Crush the rabbit bones. Add the bones and chopped vegetables to the roulades. Salt and pepper lightly, and place in the oven for about 10 minutes.

with Field Salad

5. When done, remove the roulades from the pan and set aside. Continue to brown the garnish left in the pan, adding a clove of garlic, thyme, bay leaf, rosemary, and basil. Stir in the white wine and allow to reduce. Add a glass of water and bring once again to a boil.

6. Brown the chanterelles in butter. Season with salt and pepper. Add a clove of garlic and the minced parsley. Strain the reduced juices through a fine sieve, cut the roulades into rounds, and serve with the flageolets, chanterelles, and a field salad.

Veal Chops

1. Remove the dark green portion of the stalks from the onions. Peel the heads, then slice them longitudinally, leaving the base of the stalks largely intact.

Ingredients:
4 veal chops
8 nice early figs
1 bunch spring or
   globe onions
1 lb 5 oz/600 g fresh
   spinach
13 tbsp/200 g butter
1 tbsp peanut oil
3½ tbsp/50 ml white
   wine
1 pinch of sugar
salt and pepper

Serves 4
Preparation time: 35 minutes
Cooking time: 25 minutes
Difficulty: ✶

2. In a heavy pan with butter, arrange the fringed onions in a crown shape, sprinkle with sugar, add a few drops of water, and let them caramelize.

In Provence, the early fig is the first harvest of the fig tree, which produces twice in a season. These figs might be hard to find in the markets, but if you are lucky enough to come across them, do not hesitate to jump at the chance to use them in your cooking.

Given a choice, choose fruit from the youngest branches for they are the best. Make four very light incisions in the outside skin.

You will discover with delight the succulent alliance of figs and veal. Our chef assures us that the same idyllic experience can be had with poultry or wild game.

Our chef gives you room to experiment: Snow peas or braised lettuce can replace the spinach. And if you like veal chops with a cream sauce, you may add some crème fraîche to the cooking juices.

This recipe, though extremely easy, will nevertheless bring honor to the most prestigious dinner. Lovers of great cuisine will discern its originality and distinction.

Serve this dish hot, because it does not keep well. Having well earned your blue ribbon, be prepared to bow to the acclamation that this splendid preparation will earn you.

Our wine expert suggests a Saint-Nicolas-de-Bourgueil, that great red wine from the Loire so reputed for its overtones of green pepper.

3. Remove the tough stems from the spinach and wash it well. Sauté briefly in another heavy pan containing butter. Salt and pepper and set aside.

4. Clean the figs, remove the tough stem ends, cut a cross into the crown of the fruit and incise lightly down along the skin. Place a nugget of butter in the opening, and roast them in the oven for a few minutes.

with Early Figs

5. Salt and pepper the veal chops, then sauté them in a frying pan in oil. Turn from time to time so that they remain tender.

6. When the chops are done, remove them to a platter. Deglaze the pan with white wine and reduce. Arrange the spinach, figs and onions around the chops, nap with the pan gravy, and serve piping hot.

Partridge "Chops" with

1. Clean the partridges. Bone and fillet the fowl, keeping the legs whole. Set the carcass aside. Using a non-reactive bowl, marinate the legs and fillets in a mixture of the cognac, port and white wine for 3 hours.

2. In a heavy pot, brown the bones in a little oil. Add the coarsely chopped onion, carrots, and seasonings. Stir in the marinade; boil briefly. Add ¾ cup/200 ml water and the tomato paste.

Ingredients:
2 plump partridges
7 oz/200 g sausage meat
3½ oz/100 g chicken livers
6 oz/160 g foie gras
6½ tbsp/100 ml port
6½ tbsp/100 ml white wine
3½ tbsp/50 ml cognac
3½ tbsp/50 g butter
1 onion; 2 carrots
1 tbsp tomato paste
4 cèpes
1 egg yolk; 1 tbsp cream
6½ tbsp/100 ml truffle juice
2 crépines (pork cauls)
3 shallots; 1 tbsp oil
6½ tbsp/100 ml raspberry
  vinegar
1 handful sour cherries
thyme, bay leaf, parsley

Serves 4
Preparation time: 45 minutes
Cooking time: 40 minutes
Marinating time: 3 hours
Difficulty: ✸✸✸

This regional dish is a perfumed bouquet that will suffuse your household with a variety of aromas, one more appetizing than the next.

The only real problem will be that of bagging the partridges in the fields. But you need not give up the joy of cooking game birds just because you are not a skilled hunter. Console yourself—you may find them at your specialty poultry market, and while you are at it, have the birds boned. This recipe works perfectly well with pigeons or squab. Count on one pigeon for every two diners.

If you have the birds boned, be sure to obtain the carcasses from the butcher so you can brown them with cognac, white wine, and a bouquet garni. The result is truly delectable. These partridge "chops" are served very hot with stuffed cèpes or (other large mushrooms) and sour cherries.

Your guests, already roused by the odors emanating from your kitchen, will be licking their lips even before they get to the table. And when they taste this culinary masterpiece, they will honor you for sharing your gastronomic triumph.

Our wine choice is a Chinon (Château de la Grille) made from the Cabernet-franc grape. This wine ages remarkably well and is in many ways like the great Châteaux vintages of the Bordelais.

3. Remove the mushroom stems and reserve them. Brown the caps in a frying pan until just golden; set aside. For the stuffing, coarsely chop the sausage meat, chicken livers, and the liver and giblets of the partridge. Add salt and pepper, the egg yolk, cream and truffle juice, and mix thoroughly.

4. For the chops: Spread the crépines on a board. On each place a spoonful of stuffing, a partridge breast, a slice of foie gras, a partridge leg, and finish with another spoonful of stuffing. Season with salt and pepper. Wrap the caul firmly around the stuffing, fillet, and thigh section, leaving the leg shaft protruding.

Stuffed Mushrooms

5. Peel and mince the shallots; chop the parsley. Finely dice the mushroom stems and fry them in butter. Once they are done, add the shallots and parsley. Continue to cook. Place 1 tbsp of this stuffing into each mushroom cap.

6. Sauté the partridge "chops" slowly in oil and butter. Arrange on a serving platter with stuffed mushrooms. Drain the pan and deglaze with the raspberry vinegar. Add the cherries, cook briefly, then add to the platter. Strain the cooking liquid and reduce; whirl in bits of butter. Nap over the "chops" and stuffed mushrooms.

Rabbit en Crépines

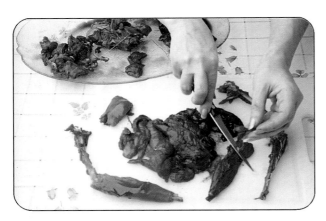

1. Bone the rabbit. Chop the carrots and shallots coarsely.

Ingredients:
1 4½-lb/2-kg rabbit
1 generous lb/500 g ham
1 generous lb/500 g unsalted pork fat
crépine (pork caul)
4 slices soft white bread
6½ tbsp/100 ml milk
2 carrots; 4 shallots
6½ tbsp/100 ml oil
2 cups/500 ml red wine
2 eggs
3½ tbsp/50 ml cognac
thyme; bay leaf
1 bunch parsley
⅓ cup/80g butter
fines herbs
salt and pepper

Serves 4
Preparation time: 55 minutes
Cooking time: 45 minutes
Difficulty: ✶✶

2. Brown the bones in a heavy pot containing oil. Add the chopped vegetables, the thyme, bay leaf, and the red wine. Bring to a boil, then add 1¼ cup/300 ml water. Season with salt and pepper and allow to simmer.

Wild rabbit is a game animal with strong blood that gives it a wilder flavor than its domestic cousin, which has been raised in a cage and has whiter flesh.

The butcher can bone the rabbit and remove the tough nerve fibers, but be sure to ask for the bones as well, since they form the basis of the sauce. Weigh the boned rabbit; then buy the same weight in boiled or baked ham and an identical quantity of salt pork or thick bacon strips.

Soak the bread crumbs in milk for five minutes before putting them into the processor. Among the fines herbs you might include basil, lovage, sage, tarragon, and thyme

The stock is made with red wine, preferably the same wine you will drink with the meal. Our chef's choice is a Chinon. If you want to add another flavor to this savory combination, deglaze the pan with cognac.

If the pre-cooking does not proceed past the mid-point, the crépine packages can be kept in the refrigerator up to two days, then removed to complete the preparation on the day of the meal.

Serve this dish very hot, with potato cakes or fresh noodles.

Whether they are hunters or not, hearty gourmets always enjoy an elegant game dinner. Rabbit and white wine get on well together if you choose a virile variety such as a Hermitage blanc. Otherwise, serve a Chinon rouge, especially if it has been used in the preparation of the dish.

3. To make the stuffing, grind the rabbit meat in a food processor. Add the ham, pork fat, parsley, a pinch of fines herbs, the eggs, the milk-softened bread, salt and pepper. Process the whole and set aside.

4. Cut the crépines into 8 pieces. Spread them out and place 2 tbsp stuffing on each. Roll firmly together, season with salt and pepper, and sauté the sausages in butter over low heat.

with Herbs

5. Degrease the pan, strain the liquid through a fine sieve, and reduce it.

6. Add the cognac to the pan and flambé briefly. Finish the sauce by whirling in bits of butter. Pour the sauce onto the serving platter, arrange the sausages on top, and serve very hot.

Galantine of Pheasant

1. Clean and bone the pheasant, being careful not to pierce the skin.

Ingredients:
1 pheasant cock
8¾ oz/250 g pork neck
5¼ oz/150 g pork fat
2 thin sheets of fatback or bacon
5¼ oz/150 g foie gras
2 onions
2 carrots
2 turnips
1 celery root
1 leek
2 chicken bouillon cubes
1 truffle
3½ tbsp/50 ml cognac
6½ tbsp/100 ml Madeira
1 tbsp *quatre épices*
salt and pepper
piece of muslin

Serves 8
Preparation time: 40 minutes
Cooking time: 1 hour 30 minutes
Difficulty: ✷✷

2. Bring a kettle of water to a boil. Chop coarsely the onions, carrots, turnips, celery root, and leek, and put these in the water. Add the pheasant bones and bouillon cubes, and simmer over low heat.

This regional recipe admirably transmits the richness of the cuisine of the peaceful pastoral landscape of the Sologne, and merits a page of its own in the culinary patrimony of France. Known for its hunting and its wild game, the Sologne boasts many gastronomic resources that enhance its native products, notably its famous honey. The masterful simplicity of this dish has thrilled generations of gourmets.

This *galantine*, or stuffed meat roll, is poached in bouillon. If you choose to bake it in the oven the old-fashioned way and serve it warm, you will have created a *ballottine*.

The stuffing calls for pork. Although you can use less fatty meats such as poultry, pork stuffing is less likely to dry out. All the various forms of pork called for in the recipe may not be available; if you substitute bacon for one of the elements, be sure to soak it first to remove some of the salt.

If your gourmet market does not carry *quatre épices* (a traditional mixture of four spices), you can create your own to taste from nutmeg, cloves or cinnamon, ginger, and white pepper.

This roll is served like a terrine, with pickles and a crisp salad alongside. The galantine will keep eight days in the refrigerator and two to three weeks in its bouillon. So you can imagine how many picnics you can look forward to enjoying!

Our expert suggests a wine from the garden-spot of France, a Pouilly-Fumé: This white wine bathed by the Loire is incomparably elegant.

3. For the stuffing, coarsely grind the pork neck with the fat.

4. Salt and pepper this stuffing. Incorporate half the chopped truffle, the quatre épices, cognac, and Madeira. Mix well.

à Quatre Épices

5. Cover a narrow strip of fatback the length of the galantine with foie gras, top with the remaining chopped truffles, and roll into a narrow sausage. Set aside. Center a sheet of fatback on a large sheet of muslin. Layer with the boned pheasant and stuffing, then center the foie gras sausage.

6. Roll together and tie the muslin. Poach the galantine in the pheasant stock made in Step 2 for 1½ hours. When cooked, drain carefully, tighten up the package and re-tie it. Place it back in the bouillon, and let it cool. When cool, slice thinly and serve with salad.

Capon with

1. Clean and singe the capon and truss it with string.

Ingredients:
1 capon
8¾ oz/250 g foie gras
2 cubes chicken bouillon
10½ oz/300 g carrots
10½ oz/300 g turnips
4 potatoes
7 oz/200g leeks
1 stalk celery
2 onions
1 head garlic
4 tomatoes
6½ tbsp/100 ml Madeira
1 cup/250 ml crème
  fraîche
10 tbsp/150 g butter
1 bouquet garni
salt and pepper

Serves 8
Preparation time: 20 minutes
Cooking time: 1 hour 30 minutes
Difficulty: *

2. Bring a kettle of water to a boil, then introduce the crushed bouillon cubes, the bouquet garni, and the capon, and simmer over low heat for 1 hour.

Capon is the poultry par excellence for holiday feasting. To produce a capon, a young rooster is castrated and specially fattened. Its delectable flesh is made especially rich by the accumulation of layers of fat between the muscles and has a very delicate flavor. These voluptuous birds can reach 13 pounds, or 6 kg!

Remarkably tender, the capon has been prized since antiquity. The production of capons is very costly and was abandoned for a time, but has fortunately been taken up again in the areas of Bresse and Landes. The commercial raising of capons is carefully monitored; hormonal castration has been banned since 1959.

So a capon is a meal for special occasions with many appetites at the table. Poaching is a slow simmering style of cuisine, much like simmering a stew, and it requires a certain devotion. Count on an hour and a half of slow cooking with no particular surveillance.

Stewed chicken, like stewed beef, has a special affinity for vegetables. Use this opportunity to prepare a beautiful bouquet of vitamins. To preserve their color and nutrition, the vegetables should cook only briefly. Add them at the end of the cooking period so they will release their odors and perfume the fowl.

This farmyard aristocrat deserves the honor of a subtle sauce made with mousse of foie gras as a tribute to his lordship.

It is only natural that one of the masterpieces of French cuisine should join one of the world's greatest wines: the red Musigny.

3. Peel the carrots and turnips, leaving them whole and in a natural shape. Peel and shape the potatoes. Clean the leeks and celery; peel the onions; crush the garlic.

4. Add the vegetables to the simmering pot after the capon has cooked an hour. Remove them from the pot while still slightly crisp. Peel and seed the tomatoes.

Foie Gras

5. When the capon is tender, remove it from the pot and set aside, keeping it warm. Pour the Madeira into the simmering liquid, and reduce the liquid to ¼ its initial volume. Stir in the crème fraîche and allow the sauce to thicken over low heat.

6. Finish off the sauce by whisking in the foie gras and butter a few pieces at a time. Place the capon on a serving platter. Surround it with the vegetables and halved tomatoes, and serve very hot with the sauce alongside.

Fillets of Hare

1. Bone the saddles of rabbit so as to lift the fillets free from the bones.

2. Crush the bones and brown them in a heavy pan with half the oil. Add the coarsely chopped onion and carrot, and season with the thyme, bay leaf, parsley and half the juniper berries.

3. When the mixture is well-browned, pour in the white wine. Let it come to a boil. Season with salt and pepper. Add 2 glasses of water and simmer until the liquid is reduced by half.

Ingredients:
2 saddles of rabbit
5¾ oz/150 g *crépine*
6½ tbsp/100 ml oil
1 onion; 1 carrot
thyme; bay leaf
1 sprig parsley
1 tsp juniper berries
2 cups/500 ml white wine
6½ tbsp/100 ml crème
   fraîche
1 tbsp butter
For the corn cakes:
2 cups/500 ml milk
1 cup less 1 tbsp/110 g
   corn flour
1 pinch nutmeg
1 egg yolk; 1 tbsp butter
4 figs
salt and pepper

Serves 4
Preparation time: 35 minutes
Cooking time: 45 minutes
Difficulty: ✷✷

The hunter will raise the hare from his hole, and the cook will raise the fillets from this estimable game animal and prepare them according to this recipe. In other words, you will bone the saddle, which is the fleshy section extending from the rib cage to the thighs. Count on one saddle for two diners.

Keep in mind that, although raw rabbit will keep for two days in the refrigerator, once it is roasted, it must be eaten immediately.

To make the sauce, crush the rabbit bones with the juniper berries, add them along with the bouquet garni to the chopped carrots and onions, and sprinkle them all with white wine. This base, reduced to a syrupy consistency, is truly outstanding. Then add crème fraîche and finish the sauce off with butter, in the classic French manner.

Serve the fillet of hare piping hot with cornmeal cakes and fresh figs which have been briefly roasted in butter.

Juniper berries with their resiny, peppery flavor are the pre-eminent seasoning for preparations of wild game such as hare. Subtly flavored and perfumed by its fruited garnish, this dish will allow you to celebrate hunting season in fine gastronomic style.

Our wine expert would like to introduce you to a red Hermitage, one of the premier wines of the Rhône valley.

4. Wrap each fillet in a crépine. Salt and pepper them. For the corn cakes, bring the milk to a boil. Sprinkle in the corn flour and stir to combine. Add salt, pepper, and nutmeg and blend to a thick paste. Allow to cool and, off the heat, whisk in the egg yolk. Spread 1 in/1.5 cm thick on a board, then cut rounds and fry them in butter.

with Juniper Berries

5. In a frying pan, sauté the rabbit fillets in the remaining oil, turning from time to time. Cut a shallow cross in the crown of each fig. Add a dollop of butter to the openings and let them roast 2 minutes in the oven.

6. Degrease the fillet pan. Add the bouillon from Step 3, finely strained, and reduce, scraping up any bits. Add the crème fraîche and remaining juniper berries. Whisk in bits of butter, one at a time. Place the fillets on a warm platter. Nap with sauce and serve very hot with the figs and corn cakes.

Wild Duck Salmis

1. Chop the onions and 2 of the carrots coarsely. Brown the duck in a heavy pan containing a little oil and some of the butter. Once it has colored up nicely, add the vegetables, the thyme and the bay leaf. Season with salt and pepper.

Ingredients:
1 wild duck
5¾ oz/150 g foie gras of duck
3 onions
10½ oz/300 g carrots
2 tbsp oil
10 tbsp/150g butter
3½ tbsp/50 ml cognac
6½ tbsp/100 ml Madeira
¾ cup/200 ml white wine
7 oz/200 g pearl onions
1 tbsp sugar
7 oz/200 g mushrooms
juice of ½ lemon
thyme
bay leaf
salt and pepper

Serves 4
Preparation time: 30 minutes
Cooking time: 35 minutes
Difficulty: ✲✲

2. Flambé the preparation in the pan with cognac, pour in the Madeira and allow the mixture to cook for 5 more minutes. Add the white wine.

Basing his dish on a regional recipe prepared in red wine, our chef proposes a new sort of *salmis* creation: one made with white wine.

The principle of this *salmis*, or *salmigondis* (doubtless an elegant cousin of the old English salmagundi, a hodgepodge stew, that lives on in a nursery rhyme) is to roast the duck half-way before boning it. This prevents it from prematurely shrinking.

This recipe can be successfully adapted to any game bird, such as pheasant, partridge, or quail. If your duck is a hunting trophy, you will need to prepare the fowl, a step more often left to the poultry butcher. Pluck, draw, singe, and truss it up before proceeding with the dish.

After incorporating the foie gras, it is essential to the success of the sauce that it not be allowed to boil. Vary the accompaniments to your taste: steamed potatoes, noodles or rice, perhaps a celery root purée. Game is well-suited to a variety of vegetables, allowing improvisation of colors and flavor combinations.

This dish can be reheated over low heat, provided that the greatest care is taken with the delicate fragility of the sauce. Whether to celebrate the hunting season or to usher in the brisk fall season, serve up this aromatic dish. It will surely fulfill every wish of the hunter-gourmet.

Our wine steward suggests a Chinon. It will have the taste of a Bordeaux and the color of a Bordeaux, but it will really be a Chinon!

3. Take out the duck, remove the breasts, wings, and thighs, and crush the remaining carcass including the bones. Incorporate the carcass into the juice in the pan. Continue cooking for 10 more minutes. Reserve this duck broth.

4. Peel the pearl onions. Cover them with water. Add the sugar and a spoonful of butter and allow the onions to caramelize. In a heavy pan, brown the mushrooms. Add the caramelized onions, then the thighs, wings, and breast of duck. Allow to barely simmer, covered.

à la Orléans

5. Strain the duck broth from Step 3 through a fine sieve, pour it over the sections of duck, and allow to finish cooking over low heat. Peel the rest of the carrots and poach them.

6. Remove the duck and garnish from the sauce. Bring the liquid to a boil, remove from heat, and stir in the foie gras in pieces to bind. Stir the sauce thoroughly, and remove from heat. Add a bit of butter and the lemon juice. Place the duck on a platter and pour sauce over it. Arrange the vegetables around the bird.

Warm Pâté of

1. Chop the cèpes and brown them in half of the duck fat. Add salt and pepper. Steam the duck breast. Warm the preserved gizzards, then chop them.

Ingredients:
1 duck breast
7 oz/200 g preserved
   duck gizzards
1¾ oz/50g foie gras
1¾ oz/50g duck fat
3½ oz/100 g cèpes or
   other mushrooms
14 oz/400 g large
   potatoes
2 tbsp/30 g butter
2 shallots
1 clove garlic
¾ cup/200 ml
   Madeira sauce
   (see basic recipe)
1 tbsp minced
   parsley
salt and pepper

Serves 4
Preparation time: 45 minutes
Cooking time: 20 minutes
Difficulty: ✶✶✶

2. Peel the potatoes and cut in thin, large slices. On plastic wrap, arrange ¼ of the slices in a pinwheel, overlapping at the center. Turn this onto a buttered plate, and gently heat to soften the potatoes. Transfer to plastic wrap with a spatula. Repeat to make 3 more potato crusts.

The originality of this recipe lies in its innovative crust. The more commonly used puff pastry is here replaced by specially prepared potatoes. They will need to be cut into thin slices to make them flexible enough to wrap around the pâté.

Once peeled, you can keep them from darkening by placing them briefly in the microwave. The heat will also soften them slightly and make them easier to manipulate for the crust. Then create a "potato rose" by arranging the slices in a tightly radiating circle of overlapping slices. The petals, or potato slices, will adhere to each other under the effect of the heat, and this will allow you to slip them onto the oven-proof film-wrap with the help of a spatula.

Slowly warm the duck gizzards in a separate saucepan to eliminate the fat which surrounds them; this should be discarded.

This pâté of duck ensconced in a potato crust is a true culinary marvel, and you will take great pride in serving it at your table. Our chef particularly appreciates its echoes of the ancient enclave of the Limousin in the southwest quadrant of France.

The wine steward has chosen for this elegant dish a Volnay (Domaine du Marquis d'Angeville). This great wine from the Côtes de Beaune, with its "nose" of small red berries, is one you will appreciate.

3. Chop the shallots and sweat them in a pan without letting them color. Off the heat, add the chopped garlic and parsley. Cut the duck breast into 8 slices. On each potato pinwheel arrange a slice of duck, some gizzard, foie gras, and shallots. Top with a final slice of duck breast.

4. Fold the edges of the potato round inward over the layered mixture. Repeat the process until all 4 packages have been completed.

Duck in Potato Crust

5. Using the supporting plastic wrap, tighten the circle closely to form each pâté into a round, flat bundle.

6. Sauté the individual pâtés in a skillet over medium heat in the remaining duck fat. Turn them from time to time, letting them brown but not scorch. Season with salt and pepper. Serve hot, accompanied by a Madeira sauce.

Braised Jowl

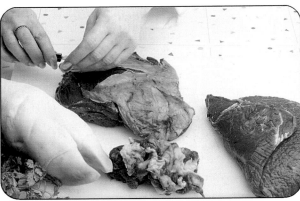

1. Trim and pare the jowls well, taking out as many nerves and tough fibers as possible, and cut them into 2 large chunks.

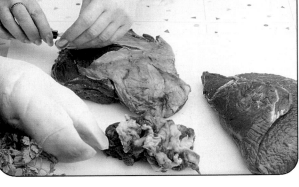

2. Clean the calf's foot. Singe it well, and bone it.

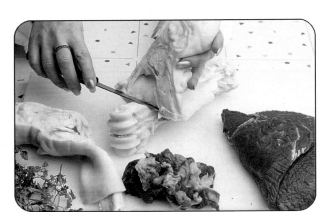

3. Cut up the onions and carrots; chop the garlic. In a heavy pan containing hot oil, brown the jowls.

Ingredients:
2 pieces beef jowl, each 2.2 lbs/1 kg
1 calf's foot
5 onions
3 carrots
4 cloves garlic
6½ tbsp/100 ml cooking oil
1 tbsp flour
1 tbsp tomato paste
6 cups/1.5 liters red wine
4 cups/1 liter beef stock
1 bouquet garni
salt and pepper

Serves 4
Preparation time: 20 minutes
Cooking time: 3 hours
Difficulty: ✳

Beef jowl is a choice piece of meat that needs to be stewed for a long time over low heat so it will remain tender and not dry out. Traditionally, this recipe required a 24-hour marination in red wine, a bouquet garni, crushed garlic, and minced onions and carrots. The jowl was then simmered in this deliciously perfumed marinade.

Since the modern cook has less time to spend in the kitchen, our chef has chosen to eliminate this step to avoid discouraging the enjoyment of this dish. Again, still with the intention of sparing you time and effort, he counsels you to let the butcher bone the jowl and the veal foot.

The dish will be lighter if, after browning the meat and vegetables, you remove the cooking oil before returning the pan to the heat. Do be careful to maintain an abundant amount of liquid to cover the meat, and aim to cook it at a very gentle, simmering boil.

To give this dish a worthy garnish, the chef proposes a mousseline of Brussels sprouts. It is simple to make and to keep it sweet, use butter and crème fraîche.

This jowl of beef will be even better reheated the next day. It will warm and brighten your dinner table and satisfy the heartiest appetites.

Our wine steward suggests a Madiran (Château de Montus). Its light vanilla tones make it the perfect companion to this wonderful winter dish.

4. Remove the meat from the pan, and sauté the onions, carrots, and garlic with the bouquet garni.

# of Beef

5. Add the calf's foot and jowls to the vegetables, sprinkle evenly with the flour, stir in a little water, and add the tomato paste. Stir and let the mixture cook for several minutes.

6. Pour in the red wine and flambé it. Add the meat stock, season with salt and pepper, and cook slowly for 3 hours. Remove the jowls and calf's foot. Strain the sauce through a fine sieve. Cut the calf's foot into small dice, and return to the pot with the jowls. Reheat briefly and serve very hot.

Chicken

1. Singe, clean out, and truss the chicken.

Ingredients:
1 3-lb/1.4-kg chicken
10 tbsp/150 g butter
3 Granny Smith
  apples
6½ tbsp/100 ml
  Calvados Père
  Magloire
1¼ cup/300 ml crème
  fraîche
salt and pepper

Serves 4
Preparation time: 20 minutes
Cooking time: 30 minutes
Difficulty: ✳

2. Salt and pepper the fowl. Begin roasting it in the oven in a heavy pan containing some clarified butter. Turn the bird occasionally. Peel the apples, cut into quarters, and sauté them in butter.

The Auge Valley is a splendid region of Normandy known for its abundance of apples. It is also the name of a method of preparing chicken using local specialties: Calvados apple brandy and crème fraîche.

For a perfect preparation of the chicken, follow the chef's advice: Lay the bird on its left side before putting it into the oven. After fifteen minutes or so, turn it onto its right side, then finally place it on its back.

Turn off the heat about ten minutes before the end of the cooking, and leave the chicken in the oven so that the juices will run clear when carving the bird. This is the secret to tender, succulent chickens. The legs and thighs take longer to cook than the breast, so if necessary finish them in the frying pan, browning them for several minutes on all sides. Once the apples have turned golden in the pan, pour in a quarter of a glass of water to keep them from darkening. To attain real perfection of flavor, the chef advises a young Calvados less than two years old.

The recipe offers the chance to give your Sunday chicken a new look. With this original approach that is perhaps new to you, you will add another string to your culinary bow and knowing palates will vibrate sympathetically in pleasure.

Our wine expert suggests a Moulin-à-Vent. The fruitiness of this important Beaujolais is a bit exuberant, but it will perfectly counter-balance the chicken and cream, and add a slightly acidulous note of its own.

3. Three-fourths of the way through the roasting, divide the chicken into quarters, pour off the fat, and return the chicken segments to the pan.

4. On the stove top over moderate heat, deglaze the pan with the Calvados, and flambé the chicken.

à l'Auge

5. Stir in the crème fraîche and continue cooking for about 5 minutes. Remove the chicken segments to a warm platter. Reduce the sauce briefly, strain it through a fine sieve, and finish it by whisking in bits of butter.

6. Place the hot chicken on the serving platter, nap with sauce and arrange the cooked apple quarters around it.

Smoked Pork

1. Prepare the bouquet garni of thyme, bay leaf and parsley. Peel the onion and carrots and chop them coarsely.

Ingredients:
- 1 smoked *palette* (pork blade roast), 1¾ lb/800g
- 1 onion
- 2 carrots
- 1 glass white wine
- 3 cups/750 ml cider
- 6½ tbsp/100 ml crème fraîche
- 3½ tbsp/50g butter
- 1 sprig thyme
- 3 bay leaves
- 3 sprigs of parsley
- salt and pepper

Serves 6
Preparation time: 10 minutes
Cooking time: 1 hour 10 minutes
Difficulty: ✶

2. Fill a kettle with water, add the chopped vegetables, bouquet garni, and salt and pepper.

Palette is a cut of pork, smoked in this case, that comes from the muscular cover of the shoulder blade. It is lean and tender with long fibers—characteristics which make it suitable for roasting or cooking in a bouillon as an element in a hot-pot or stew.

It is best to get a piece that has already been boned: you will avoid carving problems without losing any of the flavor. The length of time required for cooking the *palette* varies according to its thickness. For a boned cut, count on an hour and a half.

Remove the meat from its broth once it has cooked to prevent its flavor from leaching out. The bouquet garni of thyme, bay leaf, and parsley is essential; this antibiotic, diuretic trio of herbs is also rich in vitamin C.

The rustic nature of this recipe along with the somewhat acidic touch of cider will lend your cuisine a burst of fresh country air which, for city households, may provide a touch of nostalgia.

This wonderfully aromatic dish charms even further by its simplicity. The homespun, warm and tender preparation, served with potato cakes or steamed potatoes, will be sure to please your whole household. And it will give a special touch of congeniality and verve to a dinner with friends.

Our wine expert reminds us of the great pleasure of drinking cider with a simple meal. He suggests a semi-dry local brew.

3. Pour in the white wine and bring to a boil.

4. Plunge the smoked palette into the bouillon and let it simmer gently for about an hour or until it is tender. Skim the bouillon from time to time.

Blade Roast with Cider

5. Pour the cider in a frying pan and reduce it by half. Salt and pepper lightly.

6. Incorporate the crème fraîche and let it thicken for 5 or 6 minutes. Off the heat, complete the sauce by whisking in bits of butter. Serve along with the smoked blade, accompanied by cider.

Young Pigeons

1. Singe, clean, and truss the pigeons. Roast until ¾ done in a hot oven, basting occasionally with butter. For the filling, peel, chop and brown the shallots in butter. Mince the mushrooms and add to the shallots. Cook together over low heat. Sprinkle with salt and pepper.

Ingredients:
4 young pigeons, each 8¾ oz/250 g
3 shallots
3½ tbsp/50 g butter
1¾ oz/50 g mushrooms
3½ tbsp/50 ml port
1 cube beef bouillon
2 cups/500 ml light cream
7 oz/200 g puff pastry (see basic recipe)
1 egg
1 pinch of saffron
salt and pepper

Serves 4
Preparation time: 45 minutes
Cooking time: 40 minutes
Difficulty: ✲ ✲

Turtle doves, young partridges, wood cock and similar fowl can provide successful variations on the theme of this lively recipe based on young pigeons. The chef recommends that the bird be kept pink and rare on the first round of cooking, as it will be cooked further at the second stage. The oven-roasting must be done quickly at a high temperature so that the birds do not overcook.

Unlike the usual pastry covering for *en croûte* dishes, this one is very short—in fact, it covers the meat and the filling only partially, rather than enveloping it.

The use of saffron contributes to the originality of the recipe. Saffron is not commonly associated with fowl, and thus provides unexpected pleasure as well as sumptuous color. Created by our chef, the dish calls for a field bird which is raised in great numbers in the Forez. He absolutely won us over with his use of corn as a garnish. Be it in a custard, a cake, or on the cob, corn is absolutely fitting for this countrified but refined dish.

Once again this recipe is of astonishing simplicity. You will carry it to the table, smiling and relaxed, ready to enjoy a special treat with your family or guests. Sharing such a gastronomic pleasure that has required so little fussing beforehand will be a pure delight. The Rhône valley produces numerous wines which have a great affinity for spices. Take advantage of this quality and follow our wine expert's advice: uncork a Côte-Rôtie to enjoy with Pigeon Roasted with Saffron.

2. Remove pigeons from the oven and bone them, leaving wings, legs and thighs attached to the body. Halve each bird lengthwise through the breast bone, trying not to pierce the skin. Set the meat aside and crush the bones and carcasses.

3. Put the bones and carcasses back into the roasting pan and brown them well on top of the stove. Pour off the fat and deglaze with the port. Dissolve the bouillon cube in ¾ cup/200 ml water and pour into the pan.

4. When the cooking juices have reduced by a quarter, add the cream and the saffron. Allow to cook over low heat for 5 or 6 minutes. Strain the sauce through a fine sieve. Correct the seasoning and set aside.

Roasted with Saffron

5. Put a spoonful of the mushroom filling from Step 1 on the inner surface of each half-pigeon. Place the birds in a roasting pan.

6. Roll out the puff pastry thinly and cover each half-pigeon with a piece of pastry large enough to overlap the bird slightly. Brush with beaten egg and bake in a hot oven for 10 minutes. Just before serving, reheat the sauce, remove from the heat, and finish it by whisking in bits of butter.

Veal Fricassée with

1. Peel 2 onions and the carrots. Chop them coarsely. Stud the third onion with the cloves. Bone the veal, remove the nerve fibers, and cut it into pieces. In a large pot, brown the meat well in half the butter.

Ingredients:

1½ lbs/750 g veal shank or shin meat
3 onions
2 carrots
2 tbsp butter
2 tbsp flour
1 cup/250 ml white wine
1 cube veal bouillon
14 oz/400 g girolles or other mushrooms
2 cups/500 ml light cream
several cloves
1 bouquet garni
½ bunch of chervil
salt and pepper

Serves 3
Preparation time: 20 minutes
Cooking time: 1 hour 20 minutes
Difficulty: ✶

2. Add the onions, carrots and bouquet garni and continue cooking until the vegetables are golden.

For many years, fricassée was so commonly served that it was considered undistinguished. It was a way to prepare a *fricot* or stew, flavorful certainly, but commonplace and therefore banal. Today, fricasee has made a comeback and is receiving the respect it deserves. This classic recipe maintains its delicacy and generous savor, and appeals to those nostalgic for the good old days.

This veal fricassée is a traditional stew, uncomplicated to make, and allows many adaptations including beef knuckle or shank and—why not?—even turkey legs. In this version, the shin meat has sinew and nerve fibers that must be removed as thoroughly as possible before cooking. Brown the meat well before adding the vegetables to prevent them from overcooking. When the vegetables and the meat have colored up nicely, add flour to bind the juices.

To prevent acidic overtones, be sure to reduce the wine adequately. For a wonderful aroma, sprinkle the sauce with finely minced basil or tarragon at the very last minute.

Like all such preparations of meat in a sauce, the flavor of this dish only benefits from reheating. A very friendly family recipe, gently simmered and pampered a bit, it will fill your household with a warm and reassuring aroma.

Our wine expert suggests a Château Patris (Saint-Émilion). The discretion of this Libournais vintage makes it especially appropriate.

3. Sprinkle in the flour, stir until blended, and let cook a bit longer. Add salt and pepper.

4. Pour in the wine and the bouillon cube, dissolved in 6 cups/1.5 liters water. Mix well while bringing to a boil. Allow the mixture to simmer over low heat, covered, for 1 hour.

Wild Mushrooms

5. Clean the girolles carefully and sauté them in a pan with the remaining butter. Add salt and pepper and remove them from the heat.

6. Remove the veal from the pot and set aside. Stir in the cream and cook over low heat about 5 minutes. Strain this liquid through a fine sieve. Return the meat to the pot and bring just to a boil. Arrange the fricassée and sauce on a serving platter, surround with the girolles, and sprinkle with minced chervil.

Stuffed Pigeons

1. Finely mince the sage, parsley, chives, and chervil.

Ingredients:
2 pigeons
¼ cup/ 60 g butter
1¾ lb/800 g broccoli
For the stuffing:
3½ oz/100 g smoked
    bacon
4 shallots
2 tbsp/30 g butter
7 oz/200 g fresh
    bread crumbs
2 eggs
1¼ tbsp/100g butter
¾ oz/ 20 g sage
1 oz/ 30 g parsley
¾ oz/ 20 g chives
1 pinch chervil
salt and pepper

Serves 2
Preparation time: 30 minutes
Cooking time: 35 minutes
Difficulty: ★★

2. Bone the pigeons, opening them up from the front but keeping them whole, or have it done by your butcher.

Pigeon has had its high moments in culinary history, not the least of which is having been honored by the royal palate of Louis XIV, the Sun King, who liked to eat it with spring peas at his court at the Palace of Versailles. Pigeon has an advantage over dove or spring chicken (which are nevertheless worthy substitutes) in that it is readily available all year long. Furthermore, it has all the advantages of chicken: The meat is lean and very digestible, thus making it an excellent choice for the convalescent.

This pigeon preparation wings us back to the Rouergue, one of France's gastronomic meccas. Our recipe presents a traditional treatment enhanced by a sophisticated blend of smoked pork and herbs.

The preparation of the pigeons presents no major problems, but do entrust the boning to your butcher. Take care with the seasoning, though, because the pork strips are already salty and there is a risk of spoiling the stuffing through over-salting.

Broccoli *al dente* goes well with these pigeons, but any green vegetable or even a delectable potato cake would be just as admirable.

We advise against reheating this dish. To enjoy its wonderful savor properly, enjoy it straight out of the oven—in any case no more than twenty minutes after it emerges.

For our wine expert, the choice is a fruity Aloxe-Corton, which will harmonize superbly with the delicate flesh of the pigeon.

3. Cut the bacon (smoked pork breast) into small dice and fry. Chop the shallots finely, and brown them in the pan with the smoked bacon, adding butter as necessary.

4. Add the soft white bread crumbs, minced herbs, eggs, and the browned bacon with shallots. Salt lightly and add pepper.

à la Rouergue

5. Salt and pepper the cavities of the birds and fill them with the stuffing. Close the pigeons, and butter them well before wrapping in aluminum foil. Roast the birds for 15 minutes, take them out of the foil, and return to the oven.

6. Meanwhile, cook the broccoli in salted water. When the birds are done, remove them from the oven and add a little water to the pan to make a broth. Serve the stuffed pigeons in their juices, with the broccoli spears arranged around them.

Tenderloin Tournedos of

1. Bone the lamb saddles. Remove excess fat and the nerve tissues, and cut the fillets into small tournedos.

Ingredients:
2 saddles of lamb
7 oz/200 g carrots
7 oz/200 g turnips
7 oz/200 g zucchini
14 oz/400 g pleurotes
    or other mushrooms
3 spring onions
3½ tbsp/50 g butter
6½ tbsp/100 ml beef
    broth (see basic
    recipe) or 1 bouillon
    cube
salt and pepper

Serves 4
Preparation time: 35 minutes
Cooking time: 20 minutes
Difficulty: ✱

2. Using a small spoon or a melon-baller, cut small "olives" from the carrots, turnips, and surface of the zucchini. Clean the mushrooms and mince along with the green portions of the spring onions.

White or suckling lamb, which in France is available from Christmas through June, has been fed entirely on milk. Its firm, dark pink meat becomes exquisitely tender when cooked. The cut for this dish may be taken from the loin or the saddle, and you can ask your butcher to trim it and remove any fat and bones. If you want to treat your guests to the finest, choose a veal filet mignon as your basis.

The cooking of the medallions cut from the fillet must be a very rapid searing to make them beautifully brown on the outside, but still rosy on the interior.

For the effect of the presentation and sheer visual pleasure, try paring the vegetables into regular shapes adapted to their natural form and varied according to their different natures. Carving vegetables in this way is a tradition of French culinary art and is more easily accomplished using special knives, but these are not absolutely necessary. The analogue to this method of vegetable preparation is the French garden, where nature itself is tamed into rational patterns.

Pleurotes or chanterelles, two mushroom varieties, are welcome as well in this visual and gastronomic ensemble. These little buttons, nested within the circle of vegetables, will certainly garner compliments.

Our wine steward suggests a splendid classic wine: a Pauillac, in particular, a Château Pontet-Canet.

3. Cook each vegetable separately in saucepans containing salted water. Be careful not to overcook. Drain them and refresh under cold water.

4. In a frying pan, sauté the minced mushrooms in part of the butter. Salt and pepper them, and add the chopped green tops of the spring onions. Heat the beef stock.

Lamb Duchess-Style

5. Salt and pepper the lamb tournedos, then sauté them, being careful to keep them rare.

6. Arrange on the serving platter alternating circles of mushrooms, zucchini, carrots and turnips, all previously buttered. Place the tournedos in the center, nap everything with meat stock, and serve piping hot.

Breast of

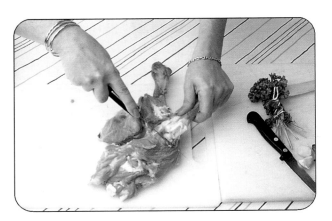

1. Bone the goat and cut the meat into large cubes.

Ingredients:
2½ lb/1.2 kg cabri (young goat)
1 large onion; 1 carrot
l stalk celery
2 cloves garlic
1 leek
3½ oz/100 g pearl onions
1 pinch sugar
2 tbsp butter
2 tbsp flour
3½ oz/100 g mushrooms
1¼ cups/300 ml crème fraîche
1 hard-boiled egg
juice of 1 lemon
2 cloves
1 bouquet garni
2 sprigs fresh tarragon
salt and pepper

Serves 6
Preparation time: 20 minutes
Cooking time: 1 hour 10 minutes

Cabri is a pretty name for a young goat. Just as with suckling lamb, this harbinger of spring is typically available from mid-March to the beginning of May. Use this recipe as an opportunity to serve *cabri* in place of the usual Easter lamb.

The chef recommends that you add the little chops and their bones to the meat in the bouillon to bring more flavor to the juices. Do not forget to skim the surface of the broth several times as the preparation is cooking.

This recipe does not require an entire animal, so our chef suggests that you roast the remaining cuts of meat slowly in the oven and serve them on another occasion with potatoes, onions, and herbs.

Serve this dish hot, knowing that the leftovers can be re-eaten the next day and you can feast again. Creole-style rice is the chef's choice of accompaniment.

This unusual variation on the classic *blanquette* will arouse the curiosity of your guests and they will be thrilled by its lemony flavor.

Our wine steward suggests a Saint-Émilion Gaillard because it can stand up to the strong flavor of tarragon, which is known to neutralize the bouquet of a wine.

2. Bring a kettle of water to a boil and add the onion studded with the cloves, the bouquet garni, the carrot, celery, garlic and the white part of the leek. Season with salt and pepper.

3. Place the goat meat in the pot. Bring to a boil, and allow to cook over low heat. Skim the surface from time to time. Peel the pearl onions and cook them in scant water with a bit of sugar and butter.

4. Cut the mushrooms into quarters and brown them in a pan with some butter. Remove the meat from the pot and strain the broth through a fine sieve. Make a paste with the rest of the butter and the flour, and use it to bind the sauce.

Goat Blanquette

5. Add the crème fraîche and allow to cook for about 10 minutes over low heat. Chop the hard-boiled egg and the parsley.

6. Using a blender or a processor, emulsify the sauce, then add the lemon juice and tarragon leaves. Adjust the seasoning. Put the goat meat back into the sauce and simmer. Arrange the meat, vegetables, mushrooms and chopped egg on a platter, nap on the sauce, and strew with parsley.

1. Peel the garlic cloves. Crush lightly and rub the duck thighs with them.

Ingredients:
4 duck thighs
4 cloves of garlic
10½ oz/300 g coarse salt
2 cubes chicken liver bouillon
1 celery stalk
1 bunch of carrots
2 leeks
4 turnips
1 tbsp pepper corns
1 sprig thyme

Serves 4
Preparation time: 15 minutes
Cooking time: 2 hours
Marinating time: 12 hours
Difficulty: ✶

2. Marinate the thighs in coarse salt overnight.

This pleasant change from the classic stew will surely delight with its finesse and originality. Indeed, the choice of vegetables follow tradition, but if you wish to strike out and defy convention, broccoli, snow peas, artichoke hearts would bring a capricious touch and amuse those who enjoy culinary surprises.

As is the practice in the preparation of corned beef or other "pickled" meats, marinating the duck in coarse salt overnight will tenderize the flesh and shorten the cooking time to two hours. As soon as the thighs are tender, begin simmering the vegetables in the broth, carefully respecting the different cooking times of all the elements.

If you have the time, try this approach with goose, but count on at least three hours of cooking time.

For a final touch, the chef suggests serving a sauce that is prepared by decanting some of the broth, reducing it and then whisking in butter. Sprinkle in tarragon or basil and nap the duck with it. What a treat!

The dish is meant to be eaten hot, but if there should be some left it can be reheated and will be all the better for it.

Offer this wonderful, solid, warming meal to your most vigorous and demanding eaters. Beaujolais, particularly the Moulin-à-Vent, is among all the wines the one most apt to enhance the sweetness of the vegetables.

3. Dissolve the bouillon cubes in a kettle of water. Wash the salt off the thighs and add them to the water.

4. Add the celery, pepper corns and thyme, and cover. Allow to simmer for a good 2 hours.

Young Duck

5. Peel the carrots, leeks and turnips and shape the pieces into forms appropriate to each vegetable.

6. When the thighs are done, add the vegetables and simmer for 10 minutes more. Serve the duck accompanied by the vegetables and the broth.

Quail en Bécasse with

1. Clean out the quail. Cut them in half through the back, and bone them.

Ingredients:
4 quail
1 shallot
1 clove of garlic
3½ tbsp/50 ml oil
3½ tbsp/50 g butter
3½ tbsp/50 ml cognac
1¼ cup/300 ml red
   Bordeaux wine
1 bouillon cube
sprigs of parsley
salt and pepper

Serves 4
Preparation time: 40 minutes
Cooking time: 30 minutes
Difficulty: ✶

2. Finely chop the shallot and crush the garlic. In a frying pan, brown the quails in oil and butter and set aside. Add the bones, the shallot and the garlic to the pan and brown well. Season with salt and pepper.

Did you know that the wild quail which scurries about in our fields and forests may have originated in the Far East? In this recipe, the term *en bécasse* means that the fowl is boned, and "juice of the vine" is simply a fancy paraphrase for wine. There are numerous variations of this recipe since you can use pigeon, chicken, or any other type of bird and choose from several garnishes: a *gratin dauphinois* made with potatoes, or mushrooms or young vegetables.

Our chef recommends rapid cooking of the quail, not more than two minutes; if cooked any longer the flesh will become rubbery. But because this game bird is harder and harder to find, you may have to be satisfied with one of its domestic cousins.

When deglazing the pan in which the bones were browned by pouring in the cognac, be sure to scrape up all the browned bits so as to garner every scintilla of flavor for the resulting sauce.

This quail *en bécasse* with the "juice of the vine" is light, and simple to prepare; it will be much prized by connoisseurs of wild game, and will provide a delicious surprise to the uninitiated.

Our wine steward suggests a red Sancerre.

3. Pour off the grease. Deglaze the pan with the cognac and wine. Scrape up the bits well and let the liquid boil briefly.

4. Dissolve the bouillon cube in a 6½ tbsp/100 ml water, and introduce it into the pan. Simmer for 15 minutes.

Juice of the Vine

5. Strain this broth through a fine sieve and bring it back to a boil.

6. Just before serving, off the heat, finish the gravy by whisking in the butter. Nap the quails with this sauce and decorate with parsley sprigs.

Chicken with

1. Peel the shallots and chop them finely. Brown until golden in a heavy pan containing 1 tbsp butter.

Ingredients:
1 2½-lb/1.2-kg chicken
12 fine langoustine
2 shallots
3½ tbsp/50 g butter
6½ tbsp/100 ml cognac
1 tbsp tomato paste
1⅔ cup/400 ml dry white wine
⅔ cup/150 ml crème fraîche
1 pinch of cayenne
salt and pepper

Serves 4
Preparation time: 20 minutes
Cooking time: 30 minutes
Difficulty: ✶

2. Quarter the chicken and add it to the shallots. Salt and pepper lightly.

This recipe is an original and succulent version of the much-celebrated *poulet aux langoustines* (chicken with langoustine) that entered the haute-cuisine hall of fame in the seventeenth century.

Unless you live on a coast, you will probably not be able to find live langoustine, also known as prawns, because they do not live long outside their habitat. That is why they are usually found pre-cooked on the marketplace, but you still can check for freshness. The eyes of the langoustine should be very black, and their carapace a shiny pink. If you wish, they may be replaced in the recipe by shrimp or gambas.

Our chef suggests a top quality chicken, free-range, corn-fed Bresse with white feet, if possible, because they are simply the best.

There are several garnishes that you may innovate to go with this traditional fare: Vegetables in julienne strips or wild rice would maintain the special harmony of elements in this fancy dish.

This is a most happy bird, escorted as it is by elegant langoustine, and its gaiety will only be enhanced by a Saint-Péray, a Côte du Rhône, which assures the harmony of this wedding of fowl and crustacean.

3. Add the langoustine to the pan and let them sweat for a short time.

4. Pour in the cognac and flambé thoroughly. Salt and pepper and sprinkle in a pinch of cayenne.

Langoustine

5. Incorporate the tomato paste. Pour on the white wine and bring to a boil. Add ¾ cup/200 ml water and cook for 15 minutes. Remove the langoustine from the pan and set aside. Leave the chicken to cook another 15 minutes.

6. Remove the chicken, strain the cooking juices through a fine sieve, and return them to the pan. Add the crème fraîche, whisk until smooth, and reduce briefly. When ready to serve, incorporate the rest of the butter, adjust the seasoning if necessary, and serve the chicken accompanied by the langoustine.

Savory Wild Boar

Ingredients:
14 oz/400 g wild boar
  meat
7 oz/200 g wild boar liver
3½ oz/100 g pork liver
1 carrot, sliced
1 onion, chopped
3½ tbsp/50 ml red wine
  vinegar
2 cups/500 ml strong red
  wine
7 oz/200 g Swiss chard
7 oz/200 g spinach
1 *crépine* (pork caul)
1 sprig of thyme
2 sprigs of parsley
1 bay leaf
5 juniper berries
salt and pepper

Serves 4
Preparation time: 40 minutes
Cooking time: 30 minutes
Marinating time: 48 hours
Difficulty: ✶

1. Bone, trim and cube the boar meat. Combine with the pork livers in a stainless steel pot or deep glass bowl. Add the carrot and onion, seasonings, salt and pepper, and juniper berries. Pour in the wine vinegar and red wine. Marinate for 48 hours in the refrigerator.

Caillettes are a typically French preparation using a base of ground meat, including scraps and leftovers, and chopped greens. This is formed into loaves or egg shapes, which are then wrapped in the staple pork caul, or *crépine*.

Our chef believes the name *caillette* stems from the patois of the Ardèche (a secluded mountainous area reminiscent of Appalachia) for *cochon*, or pig. Those hardy mountaineers were certainly familiar with the wild boars that still roam their hollows.

Caillettes were winter fare, served around butchering season, from January to March. Three days is a long time to wait, but it takes time for the meat to gather the flavors from its wine marinade. Our chef understands your probable impatience, so he offers a trick to speed up the process: If the marinade is heated before it is poured onto the meat, the marination can be reduced to 12-24 hours.

To maintain the bright green color of Swiss chard and spinach, cook them in heavily salted water. The meat and the greens should be coarsely chopped. The scraps of pork *crépine* lining the bottom of the pan will allow the flavor of pork to blend harmoniously with that of its wild cousin, the boar. The use of boar is a wonderful wild variation of this traditional dish. The *caillettes* can be eaten hot or cold, and are best with a green salad. Hunting season provides the perfect setting for this delightful meal. Our wine expert suggests an excellent hearty and full-bodied wine: a Morgon.

2. Blanch the Swiss chard in salted water, drain, and refresh it. Repeat the process with the spinach.

3. At the end of the marinating period (48 hours), chop or grind coarsely the boar meat, the liver, and half the onion and carrot from the marinade. Mix well together, and season with salt and pepper.

4. Chop the greens coarsely. Add them to the ground meat mixture, sprinkle on salt and pepper, and mix well.

en Caillettes

5. For each caillette, spread out an appropriately sized piece of crépine and place in it 2 tablespoons of stuffing. Roll up carefully, and press to seal.

6. Spread the extra scraps of crépine in a large, heated oven-proof frying pan. The fat they give off will serve to cook and flavor the caillettes. Lay the caillettes in the pan, and roast in a preheated oven for 30 minutes. Serve very hot.

Civet of Young Pig

1. Peel the shallots and onion, mince them, and fry lightly in butter in a heavy stewing pan. Cut the pork into large cubes, and sauté until the mixture turns golden.

2. Add the bouquet garni, the garlic clove, then the honey, and continue simmering.

Ingredients:
1¾ lb/800 g blade cut of pork
4 shallots
1 onion
4½ tbsp/70g butter
1 clove garlic
2 tbsp honey
16 pearl onions
1 tbsp sugar
8 mushroom caps
1 tbsp flour
4 cups/1 liter Saint-Joseph wine
3½ oz/100 g salt pork
parsley
1 bouquet garni
pepper corns
salt and pepper

Serves 4
Preparation time: 25 minutes
Cooking time: 45 minutes
Difficulty: ✳

This is a very original version of a traditional hunter's stew which replaces small game animals with domestic young pig. Prepared with Saint-Joseph wine, it originated with the river sailors who ply the Rhône in barges and boats. Add the wine—a vigorous dark red wine stemming from the Ardèche (Côte du Rhône)—and mix the ingredients together thoroughly to prevent lumps that could arise from the flour sprinkled on the pieces of meat.

The shallots, salt pork and cubed meat must turn golden, but not brown, so cook them gently. Adding sugar enhances the pearl onions' inherent sweetness and prevents them from burning.

The cook recommends that you taste your preparation before adjusting the seasoning, as the salt pork usually precludes the addition of any further salt.

This sturdy dish, rich in vitamin C and potassium, requires a relatively long cooking period, but is easily executed. Make it more interesting and attractive by decorating the serving platter with heart-shaped croutons (fried or grilled bread, in this case).

Prepare this excursion into the mysterious world of the Ardèche on a very cold day and notice how it warms you.

To maintain the strong personality of this dish, our wine expert suggests that you enjoy it with its signature wine, a Saint-Joseph.

3. In another heavy pan, gently cook the pearl onions with 6½ tbsp/100 ml water, butter, and the sugar. Next add the mushrooms, cook, and set this preparation aside. Sprinkle the flour on the meat mixture, and toss vigorously to coat evenly.

4. Pour the red wine onto the meat combination, stir, and simmer over low heat for about 40 minutes. Slice the salt pork into lardons and blanch and drain them. Fry until they begin to brown, then combine with the onions and mushrooms; add salt, if needed, and pepper.

with Saint-Joseph Wine

5. When the meat has finished cooking, remove it from the pan to a warmed serving platter. Strain the sauce through a fine sieve, return it to the pan, and reduce by a quarter.

6. Finish the sauce by whirling in the remaining butter, bit by bit. On the platter arrange the pearl onions, mushrooms, and diced salt pork (reheated if necessary) around the meat. Nap on the sauce and serve.

Woodcock with

1. Wash and clean the woodcocks, truss them, and season with salt and pepper. Begin roasting them in a medium oven in a deep pan containing a little oil and butter. Remove before cooked through.

Ingredients:
4 woodcocks
2 tbsp/30 ml oil
6½ tbsp/100 g butter
20 prunes
5¼ oz/150 g foie gras
1 piece celery root
3 large potatoes
1 carrot
1 onion
1½ cubes brown
   bouillon
½ cup/120 ml
   Armagnac
salt and pepper

Serves 4
Preparation time: 30 minutes
Cooking time: 30 minutes
Difficulty: ✷✷

2. Soak the prunes in warm water. Remove the pits, leaving the fruit whole. Set the pits aside. Mash the foie gras and, using a pastry bag or funnel, stuff the prunes with it.

Woodcock has earned itself a solid gastronomic reputation. It is one of the rare birds that can be cooked without removing its entrails (only the gizzard is removed). The famous French gourmet, La Reynière, sings the praises of the fine meal it makes. This water fowl is only available in winter, and it takes a good shot to bag the bird because of the protective coloring of its feathers.

As is the case with other feathered game of this sort, the chef advises cooking in two stages: 20 minutes in the oven, followed by a pause when it rests, covered and immersed in its juices, and then a second 10-minute stint in the oven just before serving.

The flesh will have a flavor worthy of the magic touch of an expert chef.

Prunes, highly nutritional, are recommended to sports enthusiasts and children and are known to prevent constipation. The pits, which are included in the sauce, enrich the flavor of the pulp of the dried fruit.

Wild ducks and partridge can also be prepared according to this recipe.

The woodcock is hunted from March to April and October to November, but it is in autumn that the bird is in its prime—fatter and more tender. So prepare this regional luxury in autumn, the season when it can best harmonize with the turning colors.

Our wine expert suggests a Clos-Vougeot.

3. Peel the celery root and potatoes and cut them into thin slices. Using a cutter, trim the slices into decorative circles.

4. Peel the carrot and onion, and chop them coarsely. After the woodcocks are ¾ done, add the chopped vegetables and prune pits to the birds, and sauté gently.

Prunes and Armagnac

5. Dissolve the bouillon in a glass of water and bring to a boil. Flambé the woodcocks with the Armagnac. Pour in the bouillon and simmer briefly. Remove the birds, keeping them warm. Strain the sauce through a fine sieve and set aside. Add the stuffed prunes to the warm sauce.

6. Season the celery and potato rounds with salt and pepper and sauté them in a frying pan containing oil and butter. Arrange the woodcocks on the serving dish accompanied by the vegetables and the prunes. Pour the sauce over the preparation and serve hot.

Saffron-Glazed

1. Clean the goose; salt and pepper it. Daub thoroughly with oil and butter, then oven-roast with the chopped giblets (neck, wing-tips, etc.). When finished, set the goose aside. Skim fat from the pan and add sugar to the remaining liquid. Caramelize this on the stovetop.

2. Dissolve the bouillon cube in 1¼ cups/300 ml hot water. Once the sugar has caramelized, introduce the vinegar to the contents of the pan, and allow the mixture to reduce very briefly.

3. Pour in the dissolved bouillon and allow to cook 2 to 3 minutes.

Ingredients:
1 4½-lb/2-kg goose
2 tbsp/30 ml oil
13 tbsp/200 g butter
3½ tbsp/50g sugar
1 cube chicken bouillon
6½ tbsp/100 ml vinegar
1 carrot
1 celery root
7 oz/200 g potatoes
2 eggs
1 pinch of saffron
1 sprig of parsley
salt and pepper

Serves 6
Preparation time: 40 minutes
Cooking time: 1 hour 30 minutes
Difficulty: ✳

The Orient, with its sumptuous feasts and exotic splendors, has often inspired chefs who are smitten with the promise of faraway horizons and great discoveries. This goose recipe, inspired by the famous lacquered duck, will not fail to seduce you with its original flavor and beauty.

Saffron was known to the Egyptians and bathed the gardens of Luxor in its golden color. It also beautified the plains of Israel and perfumed the gardens of Solomon. Homer proclaimed that, along with the lotus and hyacinth, it served as a bed for Jupiter. The ancient Romans spread saffron in the path of emperors and on newlyweds' beds. This "king of herbs" has been cultivated in Europe for a very long time because of its three virtues: culinary, magical, and therapeutic.

Forty minutes into the cooking period, pour off the fat from the pan and add the sugar, giving your sauce a delightful sweetness. Once the goose has finished roasting, coat its entire surface with sugar syrup to give it the luster of precious lacquer.

Choose an Indian rice, studded with raisins and slivered almonds, to accompany this succulent variation on the familiar *canard à l'orange* (duck with orange sauce).

For a celebratory banquet what could be more radiantly appropriate than the Rising Sun on your plates? Your friends, whether from the Orient or the Occident, will be touched by the exotic notes of this savory experience.

Our wine expert suggests a Bourgogne Aligoté.

4. Strain the liquid through a fine sieve. Incorporate the saffron, and reduce for 1 minute. Put the goose back in the roasting pan and pour the sugar syrup over it, coating well. Return the bird to the oven, basting every few minutes with the sauce, until it is uniformly glazed.

Goose

5. Peel the carrot, celery root and potatoes, and cut them into fine julienne strips. Toss the vegetables to combine them and season with salt and pepper. Incorporate the eggs, and mix well.

6. In a frying pan containing a bit of butter and oil, cook the julienned vegetables together with the chopped parsley to form a galette, a kind of large pancake or fritter. Serve the goose with the remaining sauce and the vegetable fritter, cut into wedges.

Partridges with Cabbage,

1. Clean the partridges carefully. Cover each partridge with a slice of bacon, holding it in position under the string as you truss the bird. Season the birds with salt and pepper.

Ingredients:
4 partridges, red, if possible
4 slices smoked bacon
13 tbsp/200 g butter
1 onion
1 carrot
1 head Savoy cabbage
1 generous lb/500 g potatoes
horseradish to taste
salt and pepper

Serves 4
Preparation time: 1 hour 30 minutes
Cooking time: 50 minutes
Difficulty: ✳

2. Grease a heavy roasting pan with oil and a little butter, and warm on the stove top. Place the birds in the pan. Chop the onion and carrot coarsely, and add to the pan. Start cooking the birds on the stovetop, then transfer to a hot oven.

Choose young partridges less than a year old, and if you have a choice between the red and gray varieties, select the red, since our chef finds it the more delicate of the two. Lacking a choice, the so-called common partridge will do perfectly well.

The cooking process is the only sensitive issue in this recipe. Leave the birds on the rare side; otherwise the meat will be dry and flavorless. As in many other recipes, the secret lies in following two steps in the cooking procedure: first twenty minutes in the oven, then a pause out of the oven, covered, in the original roasting pan. Finally, just before serving, put the bird back into the oven for ten more minutes. The meat will remain moist and succulent. You will never eat game more delicate and tender.

If you have trouble finding fresh horseradish, look for it in preserved form.

Wild duck or any other fowl, for that matter, can be prepared in the same manner as these partridges. As an accompaniment, Savoy cabbage sliced very finely and cooked rapidly, is deliciously digestible. It stays crunchy and colorful and will be a great success when served with the birds.

And remember, cold partridge will be excellent the next day. All in all, this is an excellent dish, very appropriate to the hunting season.

Our wine expert suggests a Chiroubles.

3. Clean the cabbage and slice it very finely. Peel the potatoes and cut them into very thin slices.

4. Reserve 2 tbsp butter. Clarify the rest, then pour onto the potatoes. Season with salt and pepper, then mix well, leaving slices intact. Line the bottoms of individual ramekins or ovenproof dishes with larger slices, then fill with the remaining potato. These will become the famous Potatoes Anna.

Horseradish and Potatoes

5. When the partridges have baked for 15 minutes, remove them from the oven, add the chopped onions and carrots, and cook briefly on the stovetop, stirring the vegetables. Pour off the fat and add a glass of water. Stir in the horseradish, and return to the oven.

6. In a frying pan, sauté the cabbage quickly in the remaining butter, leaving it crisp. Add salt and pepper. Arrange the partridges on the serving platter, garnished with one of the unmolded potato ramekins and little mounds of cabbage. Strain the sauce through a fine sieve, and serve it with the partridge platter.

Roast Wild Duck with

1. Clean the ducks carefully and truss them with string. Season with salt and pepper and sauté them on top of the stove in a deep pan with a little oil and butter. Turn from time to time.

Ingredients:
2 teal ducks or other
   small wild ducks
2 tbsp/30 ml oil
10 tbsp/150 g butter
5 carrots
2 onions
½ celery root
6 turnips
1 cube veal stock
2 sprigs of Italian
   parsley
salt and pepper

Serves 2
Preparation time: 15 minutes
Cooking time: 20 minutes
Difficulty: ✳

2. Peel 2 of the carrots, the onions, a small piece of the celery root and 1 turnip, and chop them all coarsely.

Teal ducks are the smallest of the wild ducks. They rarely migrate in winter, and so tend to be available all year round in areas where the climate is not too severe. However, the summer migrants with their slightly bitter taste are most prized by aficionados for their delicate flavor.

If you like variations on a theme, the woodcock and pigeon are birds that will also do honor to this preparation.

The Teal duck has exquisite flesh which yields a very light juice. It can be used to dress the carrots and celery root that accompanies it. Celery root is rich in vitamins A, B, and C, magnesium, manganese, and iron. It is a purifier of the blood, a regenerator of red blood cells, and an aid in therapeutic weight loss.

Here we have a regional recipe that could become a favorite. The simplicity and rapidity of its execution already make it a delicious pleasure. It can be served cold the next day along with a green salad.

This migrant duck usually stops off in the marshes. Invite your friends to a hunting party, promise to prepare their haul of game, and they will be happy to oblige by bagging some fowl for the feast. The hunters will appreciate your putting their trophies to such marvelous use. Hunting and good eating—these are the pleasures that chase the chills away on October days.

Our wine expert suggests a Saint-Estèphe.

3. Dissolve the bouillon cube in a glass of boiling water. Once the ducks are well browned, add the chopped vegetables to the pan and cook until golden.

4. At the end of the cooking period, pour in the veal bouillon. Allow to simmer for 7 to 8 minutes. Add the parsley.

Checkerboard Vegetables

5. For the garnish, peel and carve the turnips into regular ovoid shapes. Cut some of the celery root and the remaining carrots into flat strips. Dice the remaining celery root. Remove the ducks from the pan, strain the juices through a fine sieve, and set aside.

6. Poach and then drain the shaped vegetables; sauté the diced celery root in butter. Weave the strips of celery root and carrots into a checkerboard pattern. Arrange attractively with the ducks and sautéed celery root on a platter. Enrich the meat juices by whisking in butter, and serve with the roast ducks.

131

Duck with Lavender

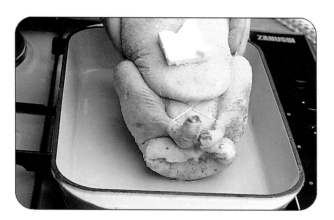

1. Clean the duck carefully and truss it with string. Season with salt and pepper, coat with oil and butter, and roast at a medium temperature.

Ingredients:
1 male duck of
    superior quality
3½ tbsp/50 ml oil
⅓ cup/80 g butter
2 onions
2 carrots
1 cup/250 ml white
    wine
2 tbsp honey
6½ tbsp/100 ml
    vinegar
2 lemons
1 sprig of thyme
1 bay leaf
salt and pepper

Serves 4
Preparation time: 25 minutes
Cooking time: 45 minutes
Difficulty: ✳

2. In a heavy pan brown the duck giblets well in very hot oil. Chop the onions and carrots coarsely.

If you are among those who are tempted by novelty, you will be delighted by this feast! Nantais duck and the Barbary variety are easily found in the marketplace. But for this recipe, try a hybrid called the *demi-sauvage* (half-wild) duck. A drake (male duck) less than two months old has a particularly tender and flavorful flesh.

Salt the skin of the duck very well so that the flesh beneath is also penetrated by the salt. Baste the bird often during cooking to prevent drying. Carve the duck before serving it. Lavender honey with its mellifluous name is pale and delicate, and seemingly more perfumed than sweet.

The taste of lemon harmonizes well with the elements of this dish which is why the chef recommends a garnish of several lemon quarters whose rinds and white tissues have been completely removed to forestall any bitterness.

This presentation with its subtle contrasts will plead in your favor. Duck with lavender honey and lemon will be a perfect good-will ambassador and bring you untold success! The Romans liked to mix honey into their meat marinades and they drank Malvoisie wines which bear a family resemblance to Banyuls. Our wine expert therefore suggests a good Banyuls or a white Saint-Joseph.

3. Once the giblets are golden brown, add the chopped onions, carrots, thyme and bay leaf. Scrape the pan and let the vegetables brown, then add the white wine and 1 cup/250 ml water. Allow this broth to cook for 30 minutes over low heat.

4. Pour the honey into a sauce pan and heat until it turns amber and begins to caramelize. Deglaze the pan with the vinegar.

Honey and Lemon

5. Strain the broth from Step 3 through a sieve onto the caramelized honey, allow to bubble up, and reduce for a few minutes.

6. Add the juice of 1 lemon to the sauce. Finish it by whisking in some bits of butter, and adjust the seasoning. Carve the duck, nap on the sauce, and serve it very hot garnished with slices of peeled lemons.

Pork Filet Mignon

Ingredients:
2 filet mignons of
  pork
4 tbsp white wine
2 large pats butter
⅔ cup/150 ml pork
  stock (see basic
  recipe)
2 tbsp crème fraîche
2 tbsp raspberry
  vinegar
2 tbsp mustard seeds
1 tbsp sage
salt and pepper

1. Pre-soak the mustard seeds in the white wine. Clean and trim the pork filet mignons and cut them in two. Add salt and pepper, sprinkle them with sage, and brown in butter over high heat.

Serves 4
Preparation time: 20 minutes
Cooking time: 30 minutes
Marinating time: 2 hours
Difficulty: ✳

Filet mignon is a cut of meat that well deserves its reputation of pampered luxury and sweetness: The middle and end of the fillet provide particularly tender morsels. Autumn is the season for pork, but this recipe works as well for veal.

Sage was once held sacred because of its many magical virtues. Its flavor, at once piquant and bitter, makes it a prime spice for meats. Soak the mustard seeds in a little white wine at least two hours before preparing the meal, as they need time to soften.

To maintain its elasticity and tenderness, pork must not cook too long. Ask your butcher for any scraps from the trimming of the cut to use in making the sauce. As in preparing any meat, discard cooking fat after browning, leaving only the juices for the deglazing step. The resulting sauce will taste better and be more digestible. For the final step, one that is indispensable in the tradition of French cuisine, enrich the sauce by swirling in either crème fraîche or a bit of butter just before serving. Potatoes *au gratin* are ideal with the fillet.

Any leftover meat can be eaten cold, but avoid reheating the sauce. Make a special light vinaigrette dressing for it by adding vinegar, olive oil and herbs to some of the pork juices. Your leftovers will be as original and succulent as the dish from which they came. This is a friendly homespun dish suitable for a gathering of friends or a warm evening tête-à-tête in front of the fire.

The sharpness of mustard is well suited to Burgundian wines, so our wine expert has selected a red Saint-Romain.

2. When the meat is well browned, remove it from the pan and allow it to gather its juices. Pour off the fat from the pan, and deglaze it with the wine and mustard-seed mixture.

3. Reduce the mustard-wine liquid, stir in the pork stock, and reduce briefly again.

4. Incorporate the crème fraîche into the sauce, and reduce for a further 2 minutes.

in Autumn Colors

5. Add the raspberry vinegar, and finish the sauce by swirling in some pieces of butter. Adjust the seasoning.

6. Cut the fillets into slices, arrange on a serving dish, and pour the hot sauce over them. Garnish with parsley and broiled tomato.

Pheasant Hen with

1 Clean and prepare the pheasant, if necessary. Bone the fowl, setting aside the thighs and wings.

Ingredients:
1 pheasant hen
16 small savory liver
   sausages
6½ tbsp/100 g butter
6½ tbsp/100 ml
   poultry stock (see
   basic recipe or
   1 bouillon cube
4 green apples
½ lemon
4 tbsp Madeira
1⅔ cup/400 ml crème
   fraîche
cinnamon
salt and pepper

Serves 4
Preparation time: 30 minutes
Cooking time: 40 minutes
Difficulty: ✶

2. In a pan, brown the wings and thighs in butter. Dissolve the bouillon cube in 6½ tbsp/100 ml water, and allow to simmer briefly.

A pheasant hen is always more succulent than her male counterpart. But choose a young one—she will be even better because she will not have become toughened by running around so much, for working out makes the flesh tough!

Unless you really like to practice arcane culinary crafts, try to get a bird that has already been plucked and drawn.

The chef reminds you to pour off the oil and butter in which the pheasant quarters have browned. It will give the sauce a lighter taste and be easier to digest.

You can prepare a fine broth with your game: Crush the bones and brown them in oil with carrots, onions, garlic, and a bouquet garni. Flambé with cognac, then deglaze with white wine topped off with water. Allow this bouillon to reduce to about a cupful. But for those who are pressed for time, a dissolved chicken bouillon cube will do the trick, especially if it simmers briefly before being added.

This recipe would be suitable also for guinea hen or woodcock, and will allow you to get a feel for an old-fashioned style of cooking which is too often unjustly overlooked. So do not hesitate. Take the less-beaten path to adventure; the hunting season is short and deserves a prestigious tribute.

Our wine expert suggests a Chiroubles.

3. Peel the apples, rub them with the cut lemon, cut them into quarters, and fry in butter. Sprinkle the wedges lightly with cinnamon. Brown the liver sausages in butter as well.

4. When the pheasant is golden brown, pour off the cooking fat. Deglaze the pan briefly with the Madeira, scraping up the bits in the bottom of the pan.

Savory Sausages

5. Add the dissolved bouillon or, if available, an equal amount of poultry stock.

6. Add the crème fraîche and cook slowly, covered, for 15 minutes. Salt lightly and add pepper. Place the pheasant pieces on a platter with the sausages and apple quarters alongside. Enrich the meat juices by whisking in butter and nap the pheasant with this sauce. Serve very hot.

Tournedos of Wild Boar

1. Bone the boar. Crush the bones and brown them in the oil. Bring the red wine to a boil. Peel the onion, carrot, shallots, garlic and celery. Cut the tomato into pieces, and sauté all the vegetables together.

2. Flambé the boiled wine and add ¾ of the vinegar to it. Add the cooked vegetables, the bones, 18 juniper berries, salt and pepper, and the bouquet garni.

Ingredients:
1 loin young wild boar
1 onion; 1 carrot
3 shallots; 1 head garlic
1 stalk celery; 1 tomato
4 cups/1 liter aged red wine
1²/₃ cup/400 ml red wine vinegar
25 juniper berries
4 cups/1 liter chicken stock
1 tbsp sugar
1 tbsp peppercorns
4 apples
3½ tbsp/50 g butter
6 spoonfuls blackberry preserves
2½ tbsp/20 g potato starch
1 bouquet garni
salt and pepper

Serves 4
Preparation time: 1 hours
Cooking time: 2 hours
Marinating time: 24 hours
Difficulty: ✷✷

A marcassin is a wild boar less than six months old. It has a tender and flavorful flesh without the strong taste so often associated with that of the adult animal. Today these are usually farm-raised.

The chef suggests you flambé the wine for the marinade to reduce its acidity without losing the bouquet. The meat must be marinated for at least 24 hours. This will render it even more tender and give it a pleasing color.

In terms of the original volume, the wine must reduce by about three-fourths. Two hours of cooking are necessary to produce optimal results.

The addition of the vinegar to the caramelizing sugar will stop the cooking process, and the blackberry preserves serve as a transition from the sour to the sweet.

This dish must be served piping hot. Potatoes are always good with game, but you may wish to do something different by offering your guests an unexpected turnip julienne. If there is any boar remaining after your dinner, serve it up again by gently reheating it in its juices in the manner of a civet, or stew. Rich and warming, this dish will do honor to your favorite guests and to the most demanding gourmets.

Our wine expert suggests a Savigny-lès-Beaune.

3. Place the meat in the marinade and refrigerate for 24 hours.

4. Take the boar meat out of the marinade, wipe it off, and refrigerate. Add the chicken stock (see basic recipe) to the marinade and reduce to half its initial volume. In a heavy deep pan, melt the sugar in a bit of water until it starts to caramelize. Deglaze with the remaining vinegar.

in Sweet-Sour Sauce

5. Incorporate the crushed peppercorns and remaining juniper berries in the caramelized sauce. Strain the reduced marinade through a fine sieve, and add it to the sauce as well. Allow the combined liquids to simmer gently for about 15 minutes.

6. Peel, core and halve the apples. Sauté briefly in the butter. Spoon the blackberry preserves into the apple-halves. Slice and fry the meat. Season with salt and pepper. Strain the sweet-sour sauce and bind with potato starch dissolved in a little water. Pour the gravy on the boar meat, and garnish with the filled apples.

Lamb Chops

1. Peel and slice the onions. Sauté them until light golden in half the oil.

Ingredients:
12 lamb chops
2 onions
⅔ cup/150 ml oil
2.2 lbs/1 kg potatoes
1 glass white wine
1 bouquet garni
1 bay leaf
salt·and pepper

Serves 4
Preparation time: 20 minutes
Cooking time: 35 minutes
Difficulty: ✻

2. Peel the potatoes and slice them into fairly thin even slices.

Champvallon is the name of a classic treatment for lamb chops said to have originated in the entourage of Louis XIV, one of the most fabled gourmands in French history. Story has it that this dish allowed an ambitious courtesan to tempt the Sun King away from his formidable mistress, the famous Marquise de Maintenon. This preparation seduced the monarch, though only temporarily, by appealing to his renowned love of fine food in copious quantities. This ploy supports, perhaps, the familiar adage that the shortest way to a man's heart is through his stomach. And the French have always held that "the kitchen is the antechamber to power."

In the southern Alps of Provençe, the area of Sisteron is famous for the lamb which grazes on its sweet mountain grass and is available year-round. This is a traditional regional dish with a noble ancestry. If you can find it you may substitute *pré-salé* lamb (grazed on salt marshes), an even more refined, but considerably more costly, meat.

The chef recommends firm-fleshed potatoes that will maintain their consistency in cooking as a fitting accompaniment for the lamb. Serve this *plat de résistance* very hot and do not worry about any leftovers, because you will enjoy a second visit just as much. The simple country ways of this dish will bring a generous warmth to those who enjoy informal meals.

Our wine expert believes that a rigorous Cahors wine will do a superb job in bringing out the virtues of Lamb Chops *Champvallon*.

3. Add the potatoes to the onions and season with salt and pepper.

4. Add the bouquet garni and a bay leaf to the pan. Pour in the glass of wine and another of water. Mix the vegetables gently together, and cook them in a medium oven for 30 minutes.

Champvallon-Style

5. Season the chops with salt and pepper and cook them in a frying pan containing the rest of the oil.

6. Remove the potatoes from the oven, place them on a platter, and arrange the lamb chops on top of them. Pour on pan juices and serve very hot.

Lamb Steaks

1. *Prepare the vegetable garnish: chop the onions, carrots, and celery coarsely. Cut up the tomato, peel 3 cloves of the garlic, and crush the lamb bones.*

Ingredients:
4 lamb round steaks
10½ oz/300 g lamb
   bones
2 onions
2 carrots
1 stalk celery
1 tomato
1 large head garlic
3½ tbsp/50 ml
   cooking oil
6½ tbsp/100 ml white
   wine
¾ cup/200 ml milk
1 bouquet garni
salt and pepper

Serves 4
Preparation time: 35 minutes
Cooking time: 50 minutes
Difficulty: ✶

2. *In a heavy roasting pan brown the bones and vegetables in oil. When they are golden, pour in the white wine and 2 glasses of water. Season with salt and pepper and allow to reduce by one half.*

In France, much of the lamb sold is raised on the steep mountain ranges of the southern Maritime Alps of the Provençe.

Though leg of lamb is considered somewhat of a luxury, this recipe is economical because the entire cut need not be used. Carve out only the number of slices you need, and the remaining meat can be used in another recipe.

Brown the bones in the oven to capture all their flavor.

Judge carefully the amount of garlic used so that it does not overpower the other elements of the sauce. If you do not like garlic, substitute a Roquefort sauce as an accompaniment. Roquefort is also a traditional native product, and so will harmonize well with the lamb.

Add luster to your sauce by enriching it with a pat of butter while it is still very hot. It will make it all the more brilliant.

If you prefer, especially in the right weather, you may omit the sauce and serve the lamb with a smooth and aromatic ratatouille.

To seal the sacred troth of garlic and lamb which has come down to us through millennia, our wine expert suggests a good white wine from the Rhône, a Condrieu.

3. *Peel the rest of the garlic, slice the cloves in half lengthwise and remove the germ (the tiny shoot, which is bitter). Bring the milk to a boil.*

4. *Add the garlic to the hot milk and allow it to cook briefly, add a bit of salt, and using a hand blender, blend this sauce until it is fairly creamy.*

with Garlic Purée

5. Strain the lamb juices through a fine sieve into a heavy saucepan and bring to a boil. Incorporate the garlic cream. Let the mixture bubble up briefly, set the sauce aside, but keep it warm.

6. Fry the lamb steaks to the desired degree, seasoning with salt and pepper as they cook. (The French tend to eat lamb very rare.) When the meat is done, adjust the seasoning and pour on the very hot sauce.

Chicken with Morels

1. Bone the chicken breasts. Season them with salt and pepper, and sauté in a little butter and oil. Set them aside and keep warm.

Ingredients:
4 chicken breasts of
    superior quality
3½ tbsp/50 g butter
2 tbsp oil
¾ oz/20 g shallots
1½ cups/350 ml
    yellow wine (Jura)
1 oz/30 g morels or
    wild mushrooms
¾ cup/200 ml crème
    fraîche
salt and pepper

Serves 4
Preparation time: 15 minutes
Cooking time: 35 minutes
Difficulty: ✳

2. Chop the shallots finely. Sauté them gently in the same pan, then remove and set aside.

Famous corn-fed Bresse chickens represent the highest quality fowl to be found in France. Close rivals are Landes, which also bear certified, individually-numbered "red labels" distinguishing them from the common flocks. But a reliably raised free range or farmyard chicken, especially if fed on corn, will be acceptable.

With such a superb bird, fresh morels are worth searching out. There are several varieties of these wild mushrooms, found along the edges of woods or in orchards; the best are the "conical" and the "common." If fresh morels are not available, preserved or dried forms will do. Good cleaning is essential because the gills trap dirt and sand.

Shallots must not cook past their golden stage. Otherwise they develop a pronounced taste that could impinge on the flavor of the sauce and spoil its subtlety.

Rice is indisputably the accompaniment of choice for the chicken. White, brown, or wild rice (either a brown rice from the Camargues popular in France or the cereal Americans call "wild rice") add welcome texture to this dish.

This recipe is meant to be served with *vin jaune*, the famous "yellow wine" of the Jura mountain region. Dry and tasting of plums and walnuts, it is produced soley from Savagnin grapes, and remains in barrels for at least six years before it is bottled. It has a renowned longevity, and is reputed to maintain its quality for a hundred years and beyond. Our wine expert suggests a Château-Chalon.

3. Pour the fat from the sauté pan and deglaze it with 1¼ cups/300 ml of the wine. Let it reduce briefly.

4. Add the carefully cleaned morels. Season with salt and pepper. Allow to cook for 5 or 6 minutes.

and Vin Jaune

5. Add the crème fraîche and let the sauce simmer at the very lowest heat setting until it has thickened.

6. Place the chicken on a serving platter. Just before serving, add a few splashes of vin jaune to the thickened sauce. Spoon the sauce over the meat and serve hot with a rice pilaf on the side.

Beef Pot Roast

1. Peel the carrots and slice them into rounds; peel and sliver the shallots. Bring the red wine to a boil. Once the wine is boiling vigorously, add the cognac and flambé.

Ingredients:
3½ lbs/1.6 kg beef rump
1 boned calf's foot
7 oz/200 g piece salt pork or bacon
3¼ lbs/1.5 kg carrots
1¼ lb/600 g shallots
8 cups/2 liters red wine
1 glass cognac
10 tbsp/150 g butter
4 cloves garlic
1 bouquet garni
salt and pepper

Serves 8
Preparation time: 20 minutes
Cooking time: 2 hours 30 minutes
Difficulty: ✶

2. Blanch the calf's foot in a large pot of boiling water for several minutes. Cut the salt pork into thin even dice and blanch. Remove and drain. In a large, deep heavy pan, or daubière, brown them in a portion of the butter. Remove and set aside.

Despite the joyous warmth of the holidays, winter remains a chilly season and requires lovingly simmered little dishes to get us through the gray days. This *daube*, or pot roast, is the regional dish of the Charentes, located on France's Atlantic seacoast, but it exists in many variations and in every corner of the country. In the old days, the stew was left cooking in its special pot, the venerable cast iron *daubière*, on the back of the hearth or the wood stove for two or three days.

Today, the era of long hours spent in the kitchen are over, and this lightened pot roast will take less than three hours to cook, but be assured that not much of this time will be spent tending the stove.

Note that you can bone the calf's foot easily once it has cooked.

The juice, sweetened by the carrots, is very light. If you are watching your weight, this dish is quite appropriate, providing that you frequently drain the cooking fat from the pan, and skim the bouillon during its preparation. Season the stew about one hour before it is done.

This richly promising pot roast is worthy of the warmth and animation of family get-togethers. Hearty and vigorous, it will bring that wholesome joy without which no meal is really complete. To stay in tune with the regional harmonies of this pot roast, seek out a reliable red country wine from the Charentes to drink with your feast of comfort food.

3. Add another piece of butter to the same pan. Cut the beef into large chunks and brown them in batches. As the pieces cook, remove them and set aside.

4. Add more butter to the pan, sauté the shallots briefly, then add the carrots and cook until slightly tender.

Saintongeaise

5. Add the browned meat cubes and the calf's foot to the vegetable mixture along with the chopped garlic, diced salt pork,.and the bouquet garni. Toss the all ingredients well.

6. Season with pepper, pour in the flambéed red wine, cover tightly, and allow to simmer slowly for 2 to 3 hours or longer, if needed. The pot roast can be served directly from the pot.

Guinea Hen Breasts with

1. Peel and finely chop the shallots, then sauté briefly in some butter in a heavy pan. Clean the leeks, cut into quarters lengthwise and then cut finely crosswise. Add to the shallots and continue to cook slowly with butter. Season with salt and pepper. Set aside.

2. Put some butter in a frying pan and sauté the salted and peppered breasts over moderate to high heat. When done, deglaze the pan with the champagne.

3. Remove the chicken breasts and keep warm. Pour in the broth from the bouillon cube, previously dissolved in 6½ tbsp/100 ml water, and allow the sauce to reduce by one half.

Ingredients:
2 guinea hen breasts
2 shallots
3½ tbsp/100 g butter
2 leeks
1 glass champagne Veuve Clicquot
1 cube brown stock
½ cup/ 200 ml crème fraîche
1 tbsp Meaux mustard or equivalent
salt and pepper

Serves 4
Preparation time: 15 minutes
Cooking time: 30 minutes
Difficulty: ✶

Originally a native of Africa, the guinea hen has adapted itself to more northern climates and has for a long time been a poultry of choice in French gastronomy. It owes its French name *pintade* to the Portuguese *pintar*, which means "to paint"—an association obviously arising from the white spots dotted onto its dark plumage as though with a paint brush.

Ask your poulterer for the breast pieces, which will be more economical than buying the whole bird and just using the white meat.

To manage the sauce successfully, the chef cautions that it should cook only briefly at a low to moderate temperature, and choose a mustard according to your taste. A good white wine may substitute for the champagne.

To accompany this dish most agreeably, prepare potatoes dauphin: Cut the potatoes as for french fries, sauté them for five minutes in a combination of butter and olive oil, press them into buttered molds, and bake in a fairly hot oven for five or six minutes. When you unmold them you will have the most succulent and delightful potato cakes.

Garnish with blanched strands of lemon peel, and you will have a charming and elegant *plat de résistance* to serve your family.

Our wine expert follows the culinary golden rule that the wine used in the sauce should also be drunk with the meal: here it is a Champagne brut Veuve Clicquot Carte d'Or.

4. Stir in the crème fraîche, and reduce briefly again. Strain the sauce through a fine sieve into a heavy pan.

Leeks and Champagne

5. Adjust the seasoning and enrich the sauce by whisking in pieces of butter, one at a time.

6. Pour the sauce over the shallots and leeks, stir in the mustard, mix thoroughly, and allow to simmer briefly until heated through. Serve the leek compote with the sliced chicken breasts.

Ragoût of

1. Cut the rabbit into pieces and sauté them in a heavy deep pan containing butter until just golden. Season with salt and pepper.

Ingredients:
1 young rabbit
3½ tbsp/50 g butter
1 onion
1 carrot
4 large yellow
  cooking apples
2 cups/500 ml cider
1 glass white wine
1 cube veal bouillon
6½ tbsp/100 ml
  crème fraîche
2 bay leaves
1 sprig of thyme
salt and pepper

Serves 4
Preparation time: 15 minutes
Cooking time: 35 minutes
Difficulty: ✻

2. Chop the onion and carrot coarsely; cut 2 of the apples into large chunks.

In the old days, the word *gibelet* designated fowl prepared with wine. This *gibelotte de lapin* is a witty derivative calling for cider.

To be tender, the rabbit must be very young. In a French market, savvy shoppers pinch the rabbits' furry paws (left on the skinned body for this purpose) to check their age and tenderness. Select one with a short, compact body and a prominent rump. Its liver should be pale and without spots, its flesh, pink, its kidneys prominent and surrounded by pure white fat. Rabbit is a lean meat, rich in Vitamin B3 and in sulfur. Nonetheless, this dish loses neither flavor nor quality if poultry is substituted for the rabbit.

This regional version of the traditional preparation replaces the usual wine with cider. The aromatic association of apple and cider flavors with those of the rabbit is delightful. Salt added to the apples will exquisitely reveal the perfumes of the fruit.

Choose a *gratin dauphinois* to go with this dish that captures the fruity perfumes of the orchards of the Champagne region in northeastern France.

Make sure to serve the rabbit hot. Once cooked, it will keep in the refrigerator for several days, and can be reheated with no problem.

This apple-flavored stew reflects the hidden charms of the royal province known the world over for its sparkling champagne rather than for its excellent cider.

To do further honor to this rabbit stew *en gibelotte* from the Champagne, serve it with a high quality local cider.

3. Pour off the excess fat from the pan and add the chopped carrot, onion and apple; and the bay leaves and thyme. Season with salt and pepper and cook together with the rabbit.

4. Deglaze with the cider and white wine. Dissolve the bouillon cube in 6½ tbsp/100 ml water and add it to the pan. Bring to a boil and simmer for 20 minutes.

Rabbit with Cider

5. Remove the rabbit and set it aside in a warm place. Pass the contents of the pan through a food mill, put this coarse purée back into the pan, and simmer gently until reduced by half.

6. Cut the remaining apples into eighths and sauté in butter. Whisk the crème fraîche into the reduced sauce and thicken over very low heat. Adjust the seasoning and strain through a fine sieve. Nap the sauce over the rabbit, and garnish the platter with sautéed apple quarters.

Panned Pigeons

1. Cut the pigeons in 2 pieces, separating the legs from the body. Remove the skin, and bone the breasts.

Ingredients:
4 pigeons
3½ tbsp/50 ml oil
6½ tbsp/100 g butter
⅔ cup/150 ml port
1 bouillon cube
  brown stock or
  2 cups/500 ml
  poultry stock (see
  basic recipe)
6½ tbsp/100 ml
  Acacia honey
rind of 1 lemon
salt and pepper

Serves 4
Preparation time: 40 minutes
Cooking time: 20 minutes
Difficulty: ✲

2. Leaving the lower legs intact, bone the thighs and pull the flesh down towards the leg bones, forming it into a rounded ham-like shape.

Honey, symbol of richness and felicity, was in antiquity considered to be the food of the gods, and the Bible describes a promised land flowing with milk and honey. In medieval times it was used in candy-making, and has long been a common table condiment.

Honey consists of about 20% water and 80% sugar, a kind of sugar completely assimilable by the body. It contains several important minerals, but hardly any vitamins. Acacia honey—it would be more accurate to call it "honey-locust tree" honey—is beautifully liquid and transparent, with a lovely straw-yellow color.

Honey allows you to preclude the step of enriching the sauce because it provides the desirable luster and brilliance normally derived from the last-minute addition of butter. This association of salt and sweet—until recently quite foreign to French cuisine—is increasingly common as chefs discover new possibilities in the combination. If you like this counterpoint of flavors, remember that honey is more digestible than sugar.

The chef suggests that you put the pigeon legs in the pan before the breast as they take longer to cook.

A garnish of diced red beets sautéed in butter embellishes the serving platter and provides an elegant note. When it comes to wine you, along with our wine expert, will find an embarrassment of riches. She recommends choosing between the delicacy of a good Volnay with its red berry tones, and the somber elegance of a grand Banyuls. Good luck in solving this happy predicament!

3. In a frying pan containing a little oil and 1 tbsp butter, begin sautéing the legs for several minutes, then add the breasts to the pan. Season with salt and pepper. When tender, remove the pigeon from the pan and set aside.

4. Pour off the fat and deglaze the pan with the port, scraping up the browned bits. Reduce the liquid by half.

with Acacia Honey

5. Dissolve the bouillon cube in ⅔ cup/150 ml water and incorporate into the sauce, or use the same amount of poultry stock. Bring the liquid to a boil, and allow it to reduce again for 5 minutes.

6. Pour in the Acacia honey and allow the juices to caramelize together. Pour this sauce onto a warmed platter, arrange the portions of pigeon on top, garnish with lemon rind, and serve very hot.

Chicken Fricassée

1. Clean out, singe and trim the chicken, if necessary. Cut it into 8 pieces.

Ingredients:

1 6⅓-lb/2.8-kg chicken of superior quality
3½ tbsp/50 g butter
1 large yellow cooking apple
4 well-formed mushrooms
1 cube veal bouillon
1¼ cup/300 ml cider
¾ cup/200 ml crème fraîche
salt and pepper

Serves 5
Preparation time: 20 minutes
Cooking time: 35 minutes
Difficulty: ✶

2. In a deep heavy pan, fry the pieces briskly in butter until they are lightly colored. Season with salt and pepper.

The natural fermentation of apple juice has been exploited since antiquity. The Latin root of the word "cider" meant "intoxicating drink." This virtue must have been prized, for as early as the 12th century, cider had become a staple for the heirs of Charlemagne, who had centuries earlier laid down the first rules regulating its production. By the late Middle Ages, apple orchards were blooming in the provinces of Brittany and Normandy, and the traditional Celtic beverage, barley beer, was soon forgotten.

For this recipe, our chef advises that you seek out the very best chicken—in France, this would mean a bird certified as a Bresse or Landes chicken—for the quality of the fowl is the best guarantee of success in any recipe in which it is featured. Look for a supplier who can offer you a corn-fed free-range fowl.

Be sure to reduce the sauce well after adding the crème fraîche. When enriching the sauce, note that in order to prevent curdling, the liquid must not boil as you whisk in the bits of butter.

This chicken dish, informal and perfumed by aromas of apple and cider, is an invitation to a festive party warmed by friendships. To truly appreciate the richly fruited overtones of the cuisine, serve it in front of a roaring fire. Laughter and good humor are indispensable to the proper enjoyment of any fine meal, and this one is no exception.

Our wine expert invites you to uncork a fine bottle of dry cider to toast this happy alliance of head, heart, and hearth.

3. Peel the apple, and cut as for french fries. Sliver the mushrooms in similar form. Dissolve the bouillon cube in 6½ tbsp/100 ml water.

4. Once the chicken pieces are a light golden brown, pour off the fat and add the cider to the pan. Bring it to a boil, lower the heat, and stir in the bouillon. Simmer for about 30 minutes.

with Cider

5. Remove the chicken, keeping it warm. Reduce the broth by a half and stir in the crème fraîche. Simmer the sauce while whisking briskly.

6. Strain the sauce through a fine sieve, then add the apple and mushroom slivers. Heat briefly, then remove from heat and enrich by swirling in bits of butter. Arrange the chicken on a warm platter, and spoon the apple and mushroom sauce over it. Serve very hot with freshly prepared pasta.

Hazelnut Frogs'

1. Clean the leeks thoroughly and remove the green stalks. Cut the white end lengthwise into quarters, then crosswise into fine strips. Sweat them in half of the butter.

Ingredients:
16 frogs' legs
4 chicken-breast
  fillets
2 large leeks
6½ tbsp/100 g butter
1 tbsp flour
1 cube chicken
  bouillon
3 white mushrooms
⅓ cup/80 ml hazelnut
  oil
10 shelled hazelnuts
sprigs of chervil
salt and pepper

Serves 4
Preparation time: 40 minutes
Cooking time: 30 minutes
Difficulty: ✶

2. Carefully bone the thigh end of the frogs' legs. Season with salt and pepper, and roll them in flour.

Everyone recognizes a frog. This little amphibian haunts damp places and calm waters, and was already a prized food in the Middle Ages, especially during Lent. The green frog, which enjoys brooks and marshland, is more flavorful than its russet counterpart, which inhabits cool and shady places. Only the thighs of frogs are eaten and they are now raised commercially.

In spite of the lifted eyebrows of the British, the Italians and Germans are almost as fond of this quintessentially French treat as the French themselves. Anglo-Saxon haughtiness notwithstanding, the story goes that the great Escoffier, chef of London's Ritz-Carlton at the time, succeeded in serving them to no lesser a Briton than the then Prince of Wales. He managed it by dressing them poetically in myth, dubbing them *cuisses de nymphes aurore*—"limbs of the nymphs of dawn."

In preparing the dish, don't use the upper green portions of the leek in order to avoid any bitterness in the dish. This is a simple recipe. The only possible problem is in the boning of the frogs' legs, an easy but tedious process.

In cooking, as in so many other pursuits, success is a matter of moderation. So avoid too hot an oven and regale your friends with this royal fare. This dish is to be served hot, but can be gently reheated.

Our wine expert suggests a Savigny-lès-Beaune, a great Burgundy which will be at its ease in the presence of this happy couple.

3. In a frying pan, brown the legs in butter. Season with salt and pepper and set them aside.

4. In another frying pan, sauté the chicken breasts in butter. Add salt and pepper.

Legs and Chicken

5. Dissolve the bouillon cube in 6½ tbsp/100 ml water. Pour off the fat from the pan and deglaze it with the bouillon. Allow it to reduce by half. Cut the mushrooms into a coarse julienne.

6. Whisking the hazelnut oil into the sauce. Scallop the cooked chicken breasts by slicing along 1 side to make a paw-like shape. Arrange on the serving platter, nap with sauce, and top with the julienned mushrooms. Place the frogs' legs on a bed of leeks. Sprinkle the platter with crushed hazelnuts.

Lamb Fillet with Kidney

1. In advance, soak the sweetbreads in very cold water, blanch, and rinse thoroughly. Bring a pot of cold water to a boil, add the bouillon cube and bouquet garni, and plunge the sweetbreads into it. Simmer for 15 minutes. Remove and allow to cool.

2. Sear the kidney in a frying pan containing half the oil and set aside. Roll out the puff pastry and cut it into rectangles 4 x 3½ inches (10 x 8 cm). Bake them for 15 to 20 minutes in a medium oven.

Ingredients:
1 saddle of lamb
2 sweetbreads of veal
½ veal kidney
10½ oz/300 g bacon, sliced
1 cube chicken bouillon
6½ tbsp/100 ml cooking oil
10½ oz/300 g puff pastry (see basic recipe)
1 cube veal bouillon
3½ tbsp/50 g butter
2 eggs, beaten
⅔ cup/150 ml crème fraîche
1 bouquet garni
1 small bunch basil
salt and pepper

Serves 4
Preparation time: 45 minutes
Cooking time: 1 hour 5 minutes
Difficulty: ✶✶

The fillet, or tenderloin, refers to the choice cut of meat obtained by boning the rib section of a lamb or veal. Surrounded by a thin sheet of pork fat, as for a tournedo, it constitutes the base of a delicate meat preparation, one rich in proteins and lipids.

Ask your butcher to prepare the larded cuts for you so as to save time, or wrap the fillets in de-salted bacon. Young goat also works well in this recipe.

The chef advises that you prepare the sweetbreads by immersing them for an hour in cold water so as to lighten their flesh, skimming the water, then blanching them with a bouquet garni. The sweetbreads must cool down completely before you chop them.

Serve the dish very hot, accompanied by a cauliflower or morel custard or soufflé. The pastry packets can be reheated at a low temperature.

This fancy and beautiful-to-behold culinary production would make an elegant centerpiece for a joyful holiday feast.

The buttery flavor of the pastry will be agreeably enhanced by a young Saint-Émilion, a warm and tender wine.

3. Cut the kidney and cooled sweetbreads into small cubes and place them in the warm pan in which the kidney was browned. Dissolve the veal bouillon cube in 6 ½ tbsp/100 ml water. Cut the basil into narrow strips.

4. Form lamb tournedos by slicing the fillet and wrapping the slices in the bacon. Sauté the tournedos in a pan with the rest of the oil and some butter. Salt and pepper them, and cook to the desired stage of doneness.

and Sweetbreads in Pastry

5. Pour off the cooking fat. Add the veal broth to the pan and simmer for a few minutes. Warm the chopped kidney-sweetbreads mixture over low heat. Split the puffed pastry rectangles in half, brush with a mixture of beaten eggs and a little water, and reheat them in the oven.

6. Transfer half of the veal broth, along with pan scrapings, to the warmed sweetbreads mixture. Stir in the crème fraîche and allow the sauce to thicken. Add the basil to the remaining gravy. Fill the pastry leaves with sweetbread mixture. Arrange sliced lamb on a platter, spoon on sauce, and serve with the filled pastry.

Minced Veal

1. Trim the veal fillet, removing excess fat and any tough extraneous tissues. Slice it, then cut each slice into large julienne strips.

Ingredients:
1 fillet of veal,
    1⅓ lb/600 g
2 ripe tomatoes
1 clove of garlic
2 shallots
½ cup/120 g butter
1 glass dry white
    wine
1 tbsp cooking oil
1 bunch of fresh basil
salt and pepper

Serves 3
Preparation time: 25 minutes
Cooking time: 25 minutes
Difficulty: ✶

2. Cut the tomatoes in half. Peel, seed, and dice them. Peel the garlic and shallots and mince them finely. Cut the basil into thin strips.

Calves nourished on their mother's milk from the Corrèzes area in France are of the highest quality and the only ones to bear the coveted "red label," guaranteeing ideal conditions in the feeding and raising of the cattle.

Veal, like pork, is considered a white meat. On some farms, egg-whites are added to the feed in an effort to enhance the whiteness of the flesh. But a slightly pink color in veal nevertheless denotes freshness and quality.

The chef reminds you that veal must be cooked to just medium, and not beyond. To keep the meat tender, wrap the veal strips in aluminum foil until ready to cook. Once cooked, be sure not to immerse them in any liquid or sauce that is at the boiling point, or they will immediately become rubbery. This recipe works as well for pork tenderloin.

Shallots should remain pale during cooking because, when overcooked, a disagreeable bitterness may develop and spoil the flavor of the sauce. Always sauté them very lightly over low heat. For a stronger flavor in the gravy, a few drops of Worcestershire sauce adds a slight bite which will enhance the taste without spoiling it.

This veal fricassée with basil is served hot and can be agreeably complemented with young seasonal vegetables. A simple yet dignified dish, it will be very welcome at the family dinner table.

Our wine expert suggests a Saint-Émilion Château Patris. The Château Patris makes a perfect companion to this preparation of veal.

3. In a heavy pan containing 1½ tbsp/20 g butter, sweat the shallots briefly, then add the garlic and tomatoes.

4. Mix thoroughly, then add half the basil to the pan and pour in the white wine. Bring to a boil and simmer for 5 to 10 minutes.

with Basil

5. Mix the sauce with a blender until smooth and adjust the seasoning. Add the remaining butter, blend again and set aside.

6. In a frying pan, quickly sear a few veal strips at a time on all sides in 1 tbsp oil. Season the meat with salt and pepper. Pour half the sauce onto the serving platter, place the veal on top, and spoon more sauce over it. Garnish with the remaining strands of basil. Serve immediately.

Duck Legs

1. If you opt for whole birds, remove the thighs and drumsticks, and save the breast portions to use on another occasion. Set aside the livers, and crush the remaining bones and carcass.

Ingredients:
2 ducks, or 4 thighs
   and 2 livers
1 tbsp flour
⅓ cup/80 ml cooking oil
1 onion
2 carrots
1 stalk celery
3½ tbsp/50 ml
   Armagnac
1 glass white wine
1 cube chicken bouillon
1 tbsp butter
3 slices white bread
1¼ cup/300 g
   cranberries
2 tbsp sugar
1 bouquet garni
salt and pepper

Serves 4
Preparation time: 25 minutes
Cooking time: 1 hour
Difficulty: ✶

Cranberries are the dark red berries that grow in cool northern bogs of Maine. They are rich in Vitamin C and pectin.

In France a similar berry, the airelle, is used in this recipe. The berries are often prepared in sugar to make sauces or jellies, and they add a very tart note to sauces and condiments. Their season, from November to January, make them a natural complement to culinary preparations of game. Airelles are very close to cranberries, but neither is generally well-known in France.

As a variation of this recipe, you may choose to soak the duck legs for three days in a marinade of white wine containing a bouquet garni, juniper berries, cloves, onions, and carrots before cooking them.

Although this dish takes a long time to cook, it is easy to prepare. It is served hot with a purée of celery root or hash-browned potatoes. It welcomes rewarming, and is in fact all the better for it.

This recipe is a refined preparation with a delicate cachet that will enliven winter meals. Our wine expert suggests a red Crozes-Hermitage. The sunniness of the Côte du Rhône will suit this cold-weather dish marvelously.

2. Flour the whole leg pieces and fry them in oil in a deep heavy pan. Season lightly with salt and pepper. Once they are golden brown on all sides, remove them from the pan. Place the crushed carcass and bones in the pan and brown them.

3. Salt the bones and carcass. Peel and chop the onion, carrots and celery and add all 3 to the pan along with the bouquet garni. Stir well, and sauté until the vegetables begin to brown.

4. Once these have browned, flambé the pan with the Armagnac. Pour in the white wine and the bouillon cube dissolved in 2 cups/500 ml water. Add the duck legs and simmer slowly for 40–60 minutes. Remove the legs and set aside in a warm place. Strain the sauce through a fine sieve and set aside as well.

with Cranberries

5. Chop the liver finely and brown it in a frying pan with butter. Season with salt and pepper. Toast the bread and cut it into triangles.

6. Blanch the cranberries briefly in sugared water. Bring the sauce back to a boil and let it reduce briefly. Arrange the thighs on a serving platter, nap them with sauce, and garnish with the cranberries and toast triangles spread with minced liver.

Chicken

1. Bone the chicken; set the meat aside. Use the chicken bones and carcass to prepare 12 cups/3 liters stock according to the basic recipe, or make an equivalent amount of bouillon.

Ingredients:
1 3-lb/1.4-kg free-
   range corn-fed
   chicken
¾ cup/200 ml olive oil
1 tbsp sugar
2 onions
10½ oz/300 g
   potatoes
2 bulbs fennel
1 tbsp tomato paste
4 tomatoes
3½ tbsp/50 ml Ricard
   Pastis
1 clove of garlic
1 pinch of saffron
salt and pepper

Serves 6
Preparation time: 30 minutes
Cooking time: 40 minutes
Difficulty: ★★

2. In a heavy saucepan containing a little olive oil, add the sugar and the onions, thinly sliced.

Bouillabaisse is well-known as the pre-eminent fish stew of France, if not the world. But here our chef uses the word in its original sense derived from the Provençal word *bouillir* meaning "to boil."

Our recipe is in fact terrestrial rather than maritime, based on chicken of the fabled Bresse in France. Thus the name of the recipe is a self-contradiction, presented with a good-natured wink towards the culinary mores of the Provence.

Slightly altered in color, *rouille*—the garlicky, peppery and saffroned mayonnaise that is an indispensable accompaniment to bouillabaisse—appears here as well. It will take on a splendid corn-yellow tint, rather than the conventional rosy hue, but does not forsake the saffron of its Mediterranean cousin as its major spice.

If you choose to prepare this dish with breast or leg pieces instead of the whole chicken, a bouillon cube can be used in place of broth made from the carcass. Do follow the order of cooking given in the directions to ensure the best possible results.

When next you plan a gala night out to the theater or cinema, invite your friends to share this magnificent dish beforehand; it will enhance the most festive of evenings with its licorice overtones.

To maintain the opulent tone set by this feast, our wine expert suggests that you uncork one of the most prestigious of Beaujolais wines—and the only one that ages gracefully— a Moulin-à-Vent.

3. Pour the chicken broth through a fine sieve, and return to the pot. Cut the reserved meat into cubes, and add to the broth.

4. Peel and dice all but 1 of the potatoes. To the broth add the diced potatoes, chopped fennel bulbs (discard the green tops and tougher stalks), tomato paste and the saffron.

Bouillabaisse

5. Bring to a boil and simmer briefly, then add the caramelized onions and continue simmering until meat is just tender. Boil the remaining peeled potato in salted water. Peel and seed the tomatoes, squeezing out excess juice before cutting them into quarters. Just before serving, add the Pastis to the bouillabaisse.

6. For the rouille, press the boiled potato through a fine sieve into a mortar or small heavy bowl. Add the finely minced garlic and saffron. Whisk in olive oil a drop at a time; salt lightly if needed. Spoon the bouillabaisse into a deep serving platter, garnish with tomatoes, and serve with rouille and toasted country bread.

Lamb Fillet

1. Soak the sweetbreads and brains in very cold water for an hour or more. Blanch them in separate saucepans containing lightly salted water and a small amount of vinegar.

2. After blanching the meats, refresh in cold water, drain and dice, and set them aside. Bone the loin of lamb to obtain the fillet.

Ingredients:
1 loin of lamb
7 oz/200 g lamb
    sweetbreads
1 brain of lamb
6½ tbsp/100 ml white
    vinegar
3½ tbsp/50 ml oil
2 shallots
1 carrot
1 glass white wine
3½ tbsp/50 g butter
1 generous lb/500 g
    spinach
3½ oz/100 g crème
    fraîche
1 bouquet garni
½ bunch chives
salt and freshly ground
    pepper

Serves 4
Preparation time: 35 minutes
Cooking time: 50 minutes
Difficulty: ✳✳

The name *Chartreuse* (charterhouse or monastery, but also a unique yellow-green liqueur produced by monks) evokes a remote corner of the country, lost amid greenery. Perhaps that is how these vegetable and meat packages, traditional and great French cuisine, earned their name, since they typically consist of homely vegetables—notably braised cabbage—meat, and game.

In season, endive can replace spinach. Be sure to steam the greens rapidly to preserve their marvelous green color, and season them with salt, pepper and lemon before filling them. The molded centerpiece of the preparation, the *chartreuse* itself, is best cooked in a double-boiler to keep it moist.

The loin of lamb is boned to obtain the fillet. Cook it according to taste: rare, medium or well-done. The French serve lamb on the rare side. When the sweetbreads and brains have been incorporated into the sauce, reduce it to allow the flavors to blend and to evaporate the excess moisture that would prevent the *chartreuse* from holding its shape. If you do not have time to prepare a lamb broth, you may substitute a bouillon cube dissolved in water. Use it to deglaze the pan in which the lamb has cooked.

Follow these many little steps carefully, and this dramatic dish with its blend of aristocratic flavors will bring a touch of nobility to your table. Our wine expert suggests a Château Pontet-Canet (Pauillac).

3. To make a lamb broth, crush the bones and brown in a heavy deep pan with oil. As soon as they start to color, add the bouquet garni and chopped shallots and carrot, and sauté until the vegetables begin to brown. Pour in the white wine and 3 glasses of water, bring to a boil, and let simmer.

4. Coat the bottom of a heavy stewing pan with some oil and butter. Salt and pepper the lamb fillet and sauté briskly in the pan, turning from time to time. Bring a large pot of water to a boil. Wash the spinach thoroughly, then blanch briefly so it remains crisp.

Chartreuse

5. Strain the lamb broth and reduce by half. In a frying pan, sauté the diced sweetbreads and brain in butter until golden brown, then remove and drain the fat. Deglaze the pan with ¾ cup/200 ml broth. Add half the crème fraîche and the diced meats to the pot, simmer for 2 minutes, and set aside.

6. For the chartreuse, line a buttered mold with spinach and fill with sweetbread mixture. Cook in a double-boiler for 20 minutes, then unmold onto a platter. Slice the lamb and arrange around it. Reduce the sauce, stir in remaining crème fraîche and swirl in bits of butter. Spoon over the meat and sprinkle with chives.

Veal Fillet with

1. Clean and trim the fillets. Wrap them in the thinly-sliced ham and tie them.

Ingredients:
2 fillets of veal
4 thin slices prosciutto
  ham
3½ tbsp/50 ml oil
1 carrot
2 shallots
1 glass white wine
8¾ oz/250 g macaroni
¾ cup/200 g crème
  fraîche
3½ tbsp/100 g butter
3½ oz/100 g grated
  Fribourg (or
  Emmenthal) cheese
½ bunch of tarragon
thyme
bay leaf
salt and pepper

Serves 6
Preparation time: 30 minutes
Cooking time: 50 minutes
Difficulty: ✶

Parma ham, generally known as prosciutto, is a particularly savory Italian ham that is aged from six to eight months. Connoisseurs are especially fond of *prosciutto di San Daniele*. It is often served in extremely thin slices with melon or fresh figs. This recipe combines prosciutto with veal to produce a masterpiece of European cuisine.

Brown the veal trimmings in just a tiny bit of oil, since the meat will cook in its own fat. The macaroni served alongside can be replaced by zucchini and tomato gratin, or any other vegetable casserole. Stuffed tomatoes would also work well, but rest assured that macaroni would also be a fine choice.

Or you may want to prepare a veal mousse with a vegetable julienne and truffles to arrange around the veal medallions. The result would be exceptionally beautiful. In any case, serve the dish veal dish hot, for its rich taste does not stand up well to reheating.

Veal medallions with prosciutto is an original way to dress up your veal and will only increase its inherent charm and flavor.

A white Rully, a lively and fruity wine from the Chalons vineyards, will be superb with this elegant dish.

2. In a deep heavy pan, brown the veal trimmings in a little oil. Chop the carrot and shallots coarsely and add to the veal. Season with the thyme, bay leaf, and a sprig of tarragon. Pour in the white wine plus 2 glasses of water and allow to simmer.

3. Bring a large pan of salted water to a boil and cook the macaroni. Drain it and rinse briefly in cold water.

4. Strain the juices from Step 2 through a fine sieve; pour half into a heavy deep pan. Reduce briefly, then stir in half the crème fraîche and swirl in 1 tbsp butter. Add the macaroni and mix well. Place in an oven-proof serving dish. Sprinkle with the grated cheese. Keep warm and broil briefly just before serving.

Ham and Tarragon

5. Cut the fillet into medallions. Season with salt and pepper and sauté in a little butter. Place the meat on the serving platter and set aside, keeping warm. Pour off the fat from the pan.

6. Deglaze the pan with the remaining veal-and-vegetable juices, and reduce briefly. Add the remaining crème fraîche along with the rest of the tarragon, chopped. Blend thoroughly with a hand-blender. Swirl in the remaining butter, spoon this sauce over the veal medallions, and serve with the macaroni gratin.

Breast of Guinea

1. Bone the breasts, cut them into thin slices, and pound them lightly. Dice the liver.

Ingredients:

1 guinea hen or
  02 breast portions
1 poultry liver
1 carrot
5 young zucchini
1 onion
3½ tbsp/100 g butter
1 cube brown stock
4 potatoes
2 tbsp honey
1 bouquet thyme
salt and pepper

Serves 4
Preparation time: 40 minutes
Cooking time: 35 minutes
Difficulty: ✷✷

2. Clean the carrots and zucchini. Cut them into fine dice. In separate pots, blanch them briefly in lightly salted water. Chop the onion.

You will notice by the title of the recipe that our chef likes pastry references in his inventions. Due to the somewhat sugary nature of the preparation, the little *profiteroles* (normally small pastry puffs) as seen in the illustration are aptly named. Originally the designation indicated a way to "profit" from little scraps and leftovers by wrapping them in small pastry puffs. By the early 16th century, the word had passed into the culinary lexicon as any little gratification disguised in pastry. Today it simply denotes the happiness of the well-satisfied gourmet!

Unless you can use a whole guinea hen, buy only the breast pieces and facilitate your task at the same time. This recipe is also suitable for rabbit thighs, which would need to be pounded a bit to break down the nerves and sinews.

The flavor of the stuffing for the "puffs" or *profiteroles* will improve if you prepare it the night before. After cooking the liver, refrigerate it briefly in order to dice it more easily. Mushrooms, wild or domestic, are successful substitutes for the liver.

Do not let the honey overpower your preparation—a tablespoon will be sufficient.

This pretty dish will enliven your Sundays, so take advantage of this delightful feast for eye and palate.

To toast this encounter of bird and wine, our wine expert invites you to serve a congenial red Saint-Joseph .

3. To make the stuffing, sauté the zucchini, carrot, and onion in a deep pan containing butter, along with the diced liver and a sprig of thyme.

4. Crush the carcass of the hen and let it brown. Dissolve the bouillon cube in ⅔ cup/150 ml water and bring it to a boil. On each slice of breast place about a tablespoon of the stuffing. Tie each up into a little bundle to form a profiterole.

Hen en Profiteroles

5. Pour the bouillon along with ⅔ cup/150 ml of the zucchini water over the browned carcass. Allow to cook for 10 minutes and strain. Reduce the strained broth to half its initial volume. Brown the profiteroles in a heavy pan with some butter, turning from time to time, then place on a serving platter and keep warm.

6. Peel and thinly slice the potatoes, then fry them in oil. Season with salt and pepper. Pour off the fat from the pan, add the honey, and allow to caramelize. Deglaze with the juices from Step 5 and simmer gently. Spoon the sauce onto the profiteroles, surround with the fried potatoes, and serve.

Old-Fashioned

1. In a large heavy stew pot, start simmering the veal shanks in lightly salted water to which pepper has been added. Be sure to skim off the foam as it rises to the surface.

Ingredients:
2 veal shanks
6 carrots
6 turnips
1 head Savoy
   cabbage
6 leeks
3 stalks green celery
3 shallots
3 tbsp aged wine
   vinegar
3 tbsp sherry/port
   vinegar
¾ cup/200 ml peanut
   oil
chervil
salt and coarsely
   ground pepper

Serves 8
Preparation time: 30 minutes
Cooking time: 2 hours
Difficulty: ☆

2. Clean all the vegetables. Cut the cabbage head into quarters. Tie the leeks together. Cut the celery into sticks, and bind them loosely together.

Let's turn our backs on gray and rainy days and warm our hearts with a vigorous boiled dinner, a kind of *pot au feu*, that pillar of French country cuisine. It will put the whole household into a sunnier mood. This is a tempting dish no one can resist. Lovingly simmered, it will chase all cares away.

This joyful hotpot will take a little time: Its cooking is long and requires practically a whole morning. But think of the old days when a blend of wonderful odors let you know very early in the day that something was up in the kitchen. Your patience will be rewarded by a successful harvest of pleasure.

No problems are foreseen in this delicious and yet economical dish; just a little care in the cooking of the vegetables. They must not disintegrate into a soupy mass; rather, they should blend, but each should emerge with its individual character intact.

Set some bouillon aside to serve with the stew. It will keep the meat tender and help deploy the aromas of the treasures of the dish.

The very soul of conviviality, a hearty stew invites everyone to partake in the shared joy of a happy meal taken together.

Our wine expert suggests an honest wine with a certain texture to go with this rustic hearty meal: a Cahors (Château de Haute Serre).

3. After approximately 1½ hours, add the vegetables and chervil to the pot with the simmering veal shanks.

4. For the vinaigrette sauce, chop the shallots and add them to the 2 kinds of vinegar and the oil. Season with salt and pepper.

Stewed Veal Shank

5. Place the shanks on a serving platter. Remove the bundles of leek and celery, and remove the strings. Arrange these vegetables around the veal.

6. Add the remaining vegetables to the serving platter: carrots, turnips, and cabbage. Put some of the very hot bouillon into a gravy boat and serve it along with the warmed vinaigrette as accompaniment to the veal.

Chicken Breast

1. Cut each chicken breast lengthwise into 2 pieces and pound them until thin and flat. Fillet the fish (if necessary) and cut the fillets lengthwise to fit within the breast portions. Season lightly with salt and pepper.

Ingredients:
4 chicken breasts
1 fillet sea trout
2 shallots
3½ tbsp/100 g butter
⅔ cup/150 g heavy cream
¾ cup/200 ml chicken stock (see basic recipe) or 1 cube chicken bouillon or chicken stock
1 bunch watercress
salt and pepper
heat-proof plastic wrap

Serves 4
Preparation time: 35 minutes
Cooking time: 15 minutes
Difficulty: ✶✶

2. For each of the 8 paupiettes, roll chicken breast lengthwise around a strip of trout fillet. Bind each securely in plastic wrap, sealing the ends tightly with string. Steam the paupiettes over boiling water for about 8 minutes.

A *paupiette* typically consists of a thin layer of meat wrapped around various seasoned stuffings, which are steamed, poached or baked. The surprising combination of poultry and fish is what make these *paupiettes* unusual.

Flatten the chicken breasts to thin sheets so that they can be easily rolled. Wrap the resulting stuffed sausage-shaped loaves very closely in heat-proof plastic wrap to keep out undue moisture during cooking. Seal the ends tightly with thread or string.

If sea trout is unavailable, you might substitute salmon, or even lobster tail. And veal cutlets, pounded thin, can replace the chicken breasts. If a steamer is not available, another alternative is to poach the meat packages directly in the chicken bouillon.

The watercress should be just briefly dipped in the chicken broth so none of its qualities are lost. Again, if watercress is unavailable, green sorrel or parsley will make an acceptable sauce.

To stay true to the harmony of colors, play on the green tones by serving broccoli alongside the *paupiettes*.

Our wine expert wants you to try the aromatic palette of a Jurançon Moelleux to go with the outstanding gamut of flavors of these *paupiettes*. The wine is truly unique, ranging from pale peach to pineapple and punctuated by highlights of cinnamon.

3. Clean and peel the shallots, chop them, and brown lightly in butter.

4. Stir in the cream, salt lightly, and allow to reduce briefly at a low temperature.

Paupiettes with Sea Trout

5. Bring the stock or an equal amount of bouillon to a boil. Reserving a few sprigs of watercress, dip the rest quickly in and out of the bouillon, just long enough to let it barely wilt. Process it in a blender.

6. Incorporate the watercress purée into the cream sauce, adjust the seasoning and bring briefly to a boil. Remove from the heat and enrich the sauce by swirling in the remaining butter. Spoon the sauce onto a platter and serve with slices of paupiette bathed in watercress sauce. Garnish with sprigs of watercress.

No-Frills Roast

1. Bone the saddle of lamb and remove the fat from the kidneys. Season the interior of the saddle with salt and pepper. Crush the bones.

2. Reconstitute the saddle, roll and tie it, tucking a bay leaf under the string. Clean the carrot and onion, and cut them into little sticks.

3. Put the saddle in a roasting pan. Season with salt and pepper. Add a bit of butter to the pan, sprinkle on some oil and roast in a hot oven for 10 minutes. Make up a bouquet garni.

Ingredients:
2½ lb/1.2 kg saddle of lamb
2 lamb kidneys
1 carrot
1 onion
3½ tbsp/100 g butter
6½ tbsp/100 ml vinaigrette
3 tbsp cooking oil
1 glass white wine
bay leaf
1 bouquet garni
thyme
fresh tarragon
1 bunch watercress
salt and white pepper

Serves 6
Preparation time: 20 minutes
Cooking time: 30 minutes
Difficulty: ✳

Here is a light dish that can be the centerpiece of a sumptuous meal or a simple dinner *en tête à tête*.

If you have the saddle boned by your butcher, be sure to take home the bones and trimmings, as they are essential for preparing the sauce.

Season the inner surface of the meat with salt and pepper before closing and tying it. This is important because the lamb would be quite flavorless without it. A little thyme should be added for the same reason.

To keep the meat tender, frequent and thorough basting is necessary. When it has finished roasting, rather than carve it immediately, let the roast rest for at least 15 minutes so that it can gather its juices. This will improve the taste and the texture.

Eggplant *au gratin* is the accompaniment of choice for this dish.

In the best cooking, lightness can be achieved without loss of flavor. The alliance of fresh tarragon, lamb, and watercress is sublime. Once you have tried it, you may never use any other herbs with lamb!

Our wine expert is firm in his choice of a marvelous Chinon (Clos de l'Écho) to drink with the roast lamb. These remarkable red wines age most gracefully.

4. Remove the roast from the oven. Add the crushed bones and trimmings along with the onion, carrot, and bouquet garni to the roasting pan. Brown in the oven for another 10 minutes or so. Prepare a vinaigrette from vinegar seasoned with salt, pepper, thyme, and tarragon.

Saddle of Lamb

5. Remove the meat, but not the vegetables, from the pan and set aside. Pour off the fat and deglaze with the white wine. Add 2 glasses of water, salt and pepper, and simmer on top of the stove for about 15 minutes. Cut the kidneys in half lengthwise, and sear them on their rounded sides in a pan with some oil.

6. Just before serving, slice the lamb and arrange it on a warm serving platter. Strain the roasting juices through a fine sieve and reduce briefly. Remove the sauce from the heat and swirl in butter. Serve the roast garnished with kidneys and watercress, accompanied by the vinaigrette.

Tournedos

1. Bring the milk to a boil in a saucepan. Add salt and pepper and grate in some nutmeg. Sprinkle in the semolina, mixing vigorously. Allow to cook until the preparation thickens to a paste. When slightly cooled, beat in the eggs.

2. On a lightly greased baking sheet, spread the dough with a spatula to a thickness of roughly ½ in/1 cm. Allow it to cool in the refrigerator.

Ingredients:
4 tournedos, each
  3½ oz/100 g
2 cups/500 ml milk
1 cup/125 g fine
  semolina
2 eggs
3½ tbsp/100 g butter
2 tbsp oil
1 glass red wine
1 glass concentrated
  broth
4 mushrooms
nutmeg
salt, pepper

Serves 4
Preparation time: 30 minutes
Cooking time: 20 minutes
Difficulty: ✷✷✷

Do not be misled by the name of this recipe! These succulent tournedos are meant to be served hot with a delectable sauce—they are most emphatically not meant as snacks or picnic fare!

To make this delightful dish, be careful to sear the tournedos briefly at a high temperature to keep them very rare in the center. If you like meat that is medium or well-done, opt instead for veal or pork filet mignon.

Roman style gnocchi work very well alongside these delicate pieces of meat, but they too need to be seared on both sides to keep them from softening too quickly in the sauce when is poured over the meat.

Tournedos Sandwich Style is a dish that will cheer up your everyday meals with a touch of fantasy. Tournedos are low-fat cut of beef, and are perfect for a light meal. They must be served very hot immediately after cooking. They suffer from reheating, as the meat will turn tough.

Our wine expert thinks that the rustic nature of gnocchi requires a wine that is tender and forceful at the same time. His choice is a Savigny-lès-Beaune.

3. Using a cookie-cutter, cut 8 rounds of dough and fry them on both sides in 2 tbsp butter. Add salt and pepper.

4. In a frying pan containing a very small amount of oil and butter, sear the tournedos very quickly, leaving the centers quite rare. Remove them and set aside. Pour in the red wine, allow to reduce by half and add the broth concentrate.

Sandwich-Style

5. Let the sauce boil up a few seconds, turn off the heat, then swirl in the rest of the butter in pieces.

6. Form the sandwiches by placing a tournedo on a gnocchi, and then topping with another gnocchi. Spoon the hot sauce over the "sandwiches," and garnish with poached mushrooms.

Young Pigeons

Ingredients:
4 young pigeons
4 slices Canadian
 bacon or ham
10 tbsp/150 g butter
2½ tbsp/40 ml peanut
 oil
1 shallot
1¼ cup/300 ml good
 red Bordeaux
14 oz/400 g wild
 mushrooms
1 tbsp mixed herbs
salt and pepper

1. Clean the pigeons very well, singe and truss them. Season with salt and pepper. Sauté well on all sides in a heavy pan over medium heat, turning frequently, in 2½ tbsp/40 g butter and 1 tbsp of the oil.

Serves 4
Preparation time: 20 minutes
Cooking time: 30 minutes
Difficulty: ✶

Young pigeons are used in this fancy recipe because they are particularly tender. They have the same qualities as chicken and are both easily digestible and rich in protein. This dish, worthy of a Pope, harks back to the culinary traditions of great royal banquets prepared to honor and delight high-ranking personages.

Quail and doves can be prepared in the same manner. This dish is perfumed with a smoky bacon and is easy and quick to prepare. It is served hot accompanied by a zucchini gratin and wild mushrooms.

These pigeons take well to reheating and will keep two or three days in the refrigerator. Even if you don't know exactly when to expect your guests, these blessed little pigeons are just the thing to give them a divine welcome, for most of the preparation can be done in advance.

Our wine expert suggests a meaty Saint-Émilion to go with this respectable autumnal treat, and the name of his selection continues patriarchal note of the dish: Château Patris.

2. Chop the shallot, and slice the ham.

3. When the birds are almost done, sprinkle on the chopped shallot, stir, add the slices of ham, and continue cooking.

4. Sprinkle the mixed herbs over the pigeons, turn off the heat, cover closely and let the herbal aromas imbue the birds for about 5 minutes.

Papal-Style

5. Pour in the red wine, stir, cover again, and simmer gently for about 15 minutes. Uncover the pan, allow the sauce to reduce briefly, and enrich it by swirling in 3½ tbsp/50 g of butter.

6. In a frying pan, sauté the mushrooms in the remaining butter. Season with salt and pepper. Place the pigeons on the serving platter. Arrange the bacon and mushrooms around them and spoon the sauce over everything.

Grilled Chicken

1. Cut 1 lime into very thin slices. Clean and singe the chicken. Loosen the skin from the body but do not pierce it. Slide the lime slices under the skin, reaching as far as possible to insert them around the body. Truss the bird.

2. Melt a little butter in a large heavy roasting pan. Season the bird with salt and pepper. Pan-roast it, basting it often with its juices.

3. Mince the tarragon and parsley finely. Chop the chives, and cut the peel from a second lime into little strips. Press the juice from the lime and set aside. Blanch the lime peel until somewhat softened. Peel the other 2 limes completely and cut into segments. Set aside.

Ingredients:
1 chicken, about
   4¼ lb/1.9 kg
4 limes
13 tbsp/200 g butter
1 cube beef bouillon
   or ⅔ cup/150 ml
   beef stock (see
   basic recipe)
1 sprig of tarragon
1 bunch of parsley
1 bunch of chives
salt and pepper

Serves 6
Preparation time: 15 minutes
Cooking time: 40 minutes
Difficulty: ✶

This chicken recipe has an exciting exotic flair that comes straight from the tropics. The alliance of chicken and lime harmonizes perfectly and offers an entirely new taste sensation.

To achieve this marvelous antiphony of flavors, the chef recommends top of the line meat: a plump, corn-fed, free-range fowl (in France, this means a white Bresse or a black-footed Landais).

The trickiest part of this preparation is lifting the skin free from the flesh of the chicken without tearing it.Begin at the neck and proceed gently, using your fingers to carefully separate the skin from the underlying fat and flesh. Also take care that the skin does not rupture during cooking; do not use a fork or any implement that might pierce this golden cover. Frequent basting will promote browning and crispness.

As for the cooking time, the chef has a good tip. Turn the bird over and check the juices that escape from the rump: If they are red or rosy, that indicates that the chicken is not yet done. When the juices run clear the bird is done.

This meal can also be prepared in advance, refrigerated, and then enjoyed at room temperature; it makes an ideal picnic. The citrus flavor, a surprisingly delicious note, must not overpower that of the bird. Serve a crisp green salad with the cold chicken. If hot, it would prefer to wear a crown of lovely fresh vegetables in season.

Our wine expert recommends a dry Vouvray, Domaine G. Huet.

4. Dissolve the bouillon cube in ⅔ cup/150 ml water. When the chicken is done, remove it to a warm place. Degrease the pan and deglaze it with the bouillon (or stock) and lime juice, scraping up the bits in the pan.

with Lime

5. After a brief reduction of the bouillon, strain it through a fine sieve into a saucepan. Add the finely chopped herbs and chives to the hot broth.

6. Enrich the broth by swirling in bits of butter. Place the chicken on a serving platter, spoon the sauce over it, and garnish with the lime zest and quarters.

Beef Fillet with

Ingredients:
1¾ lb/800 g beef fillet
48 snails without their
   shells
1 onion
1 carrot
2 tbsp/30 ml oil
1 head Boston
   lettuce
1 head garlic
3½ tbsp/100 g butter
1 glass white wine
1 bunch Italian
   parsley
salt and pepper

Serves 4
Preparation time: 20 minutes
Cooking time: 30 minutes
Difficulty: ✳

1. Peel and dice the onion and carrot. In a deep heavy pan, heat some oil and brown the tightly rolled and tied fillet. Season with salt and pepper. Add the diced vegetables to the pan and sauté over low heat.

In the Roussillon, a mountainous area at the eastern end of France's border with Spain, there is a tradition called the *cargolade*. It is something like the American pig or rib roast or clam bake, except that the central attraction is snails. On Easter Monday or Pentecost, crowds gather to gorge on snails roasted in a bed of grape-vine embers. They are eaten on thick slices of bread spread with *aioli* (garlic mayonnaise) or parsley butter.

Our Catalan chef, faithful to his ancestral customs, contrived this combination of red meat and *petits-gris*, the local gray snails gathered traditionally by children and older people during and after rainstorms. The refinement of this perfect combination, (somewhat suggestive of our "surf and turf") will impress you.

Any tender cut of beef, such as sirloin or rump, can replace the fillet, as long as it can be served as slices of rare beef in a savory sauce. Wait until the last minute to poach the lettuce leaves so that they stay bright green. The recipe requires fairly heavy seasoning, so do not hesitate to be generous with cayenne or pepper.

The preparation of this dish is easy and quick. Although not authentically traditional, it nevertheless has a regional personality as it congenially joins together two familiar elements of Catalan gastronomy.

Serve the dish hot. Its powerful flavors will help you celebrate Easter.

The black robe and spicy aromas of an impressive local wine, the Château de Jau (Côtes-du-Roussillon), will be delightfully appropriate.

2. Clean and wash the lettuce and slice it through the head so as to form fine strips. Chop the garlic and parsley. Salt and pepper the snails and brown them in a frying pan with some butter.

3. Add the chopped parsley and garlic to the pan with the snails and continue to cook.

4. Remove the beef fillet from the pan. Pour off the fat and deglaze with the white wine, scraping the pan well.

Ragoût of Snail

5. Add the snail mixture to the pan with the reduced juices and reheat.

6. Toss the lettuce into the pan, stir, and sauté a few minutes. Slice the beef and serve accompanied by the fried snails in sauce.

Pickled Duck

1. Separate the legs, breast, and wings of the duck. Bone the breast and crush the carcass.

Ingredients:
1 plump duck
6½ lbs/3 kg duck fat
1 carrot
1 onion
1 leek
1 stalk celery
2 tomatoes
1 clove garlic
1¼ cups/300 ml verjuice
   with sediment
1 bouquet garni
5 juniper berries
1¾ lbs/750 g potatoes
coarse salt
pepper

Serves 4
Preparation time: 40 minutes
Cooking time: 2 hours 30 minutes
Marinating time: 24 hours
Difficulty: ✳

2. Marinate the duck by coating it liberally with coarse salt, and letting it rest in a covered bowl with the bouquet garni and the juniper berries, refrigerated, for about 24 hours.

This richly traditional dish takes us to the heart of the Périgord region. The recipe requires lengthy cooking at a very slight simmer, so save it for days when you have time at your disposal.

The marinade consists of coarse salt and herbs, and is an important element in assuring the success of this meal. Twenty-four hours are needed for it to work effectively.

The fat in which the duck cooks must never bubble. The cooking process must be extremely slow for the duck to remain tender and succulent. This patient nurturing is what produces the cachet and superb quality of this prime example of French cuisine.

The roasting phase is important to assure a crisp skin and the release of excess fat. The *verjus*, or verjuice, is a sour wine made by fermenting the juice of immature or imperfectly-ripened grapes. Though rare in cooking, it is sometimes added to the wine-making process to reduce sweetness. Its raw acidity balances the fattiness of the duck.

Remember that duck is a rich and nourishing meat which contains important amounts of phosphorus, potassium, and Vitamin B-3.

Serve this dish very hot. The duck will keep for a week in its fat, in the refrigerator This recipe should be the centerpiece of gala celebrations or prestigious dinners.

Our wine expert suggests a Château de Montus, since a Madiran is the inseparable companion of preserved duck. You will be astonished by its virility and elegance.

3. The next day, allow the marinade to come to room temperature. Remove the pieces of duck from the marinade and rinse. Heat the duck fat over low heat, lay the pieces of duck in the pan, and cook over very low heat. The fat must never reach the boiling point.

4. Clean and prepare the carrot, onion, leek, celery, tomatoes, and garlic. Cut them into a mirepoix.

with Verjus

5. Brown the duck carcass in a frying pan until it is well colored. Add all the vegetables, mix well, and season with salt and pepper. Pour in water to cover the contents, then add half the verjuice and simmer for about 20 minutes.

6. When the duck pieces are tender, remove from the fat and broil until crisp and brown. Strain the liquid from Step 5 through a fine sieve into a saucepan, add the remaining verjuice with its sediment, and heat. Arrange the duck on a serving platter, pour the sauce over the pieces, and serve with fried potatoes.

Pork Filet Mignon with

1. Trim the pork filet and slice it into ¾-in/2-cm medallions. Slice the zucchini into small oblong chunks. Chop the onion, and cut the ginger into a fine julienne. In a deep heavy pan brown the onions in a little butter.

Ingredients:
1 filet mignon of pork
4 zucchini
1 onion
1 ginger root
3½ tbsp/100 g butter
1 tbsp honey
1 clove garlic
1 tbsp red-wine vinegar
6½ tbsp/100 ml white wine
1 cube veal bouillon
6½ tbsp/100 ml raspberry vinegar
1 tbsp curry
salt and pepper

Serves 4
Preparation time: 40 minutes
Cooking time: 40 minutes
Difficulty: ✲✲

2. When the onions are almost done, add the zucchini and mix well. Blanch the ginger in 2 or 3 successive changes of water.

Few people are aware that ginger, botanically speaking, is a distant cousin of the orchid. It originated in eastern India, a country fabulously rich in spices and the land of dreams for early travelers. The Latin name for ginger, *lingiber*, comes from the Sanskrit *sringravera*.

Ginger has long been recognized for its medicinal properties and its reputation continues to increase. It is certainly a powerful aid to the digestion, and is currently growing in popularity as a culinary ingredient among gourmets around the world.

In this recipe, the chef dilutes the flavor of the ginger somewhat by blanching the fresh ginger root. If you prefer a stronger note, simply omit this step.

If you prefer lamb or veal to pork, this dish will provide the same succulent delight.

The pork may be served cold but not the zucchini, which needs to be hot.

This is an unusual sweet-and-sour preparation and requires a somewhat adventurous palate, one that is not afraid of surprises and likes to travel the world. Those among your more curious friends with exotic tastes will surely be pleased by this excursion into another world of flavors.

Ginger is not as exuberant as one might think, and the great white wines from the Rhône Valley harmonize very well with it. Our wine expert proposes a white Saint-Joseph.

3. Add the honey, garlic, and curry and a pinch of the slivered ginger to the vegetables. Continue cooking over moderate heat, stirring often. Season lightly with salt and pepper . Pour in the red-wine vinegar and the white wine.

4. While the vegetables are cooking, sauté the lightly seasoned pork medallions in a little butter.

Ginger and Zucchini

5. Dissolve the bouillon cube in ⅔ cup/150 ml boiling water. Pour the fat from the frying pan in which the pork has cooked, then deglaze it with the raspberry vinegar.

6. Pour in the bouillon, scraping the pan. Reduce briefly and add the ginger. Off the heat, swirl the rest of the butter into the hot liquid. Remove the ginger. Arrange the pork medallions on a serving platter and spoon the sauce over them. Garnish with slivered ginger, and serve with the sautéed zucchini and onions.

Roast Guinea

1. Clean, singe, and trim the guinea hen. Truss it and put it aside. Wash the leeks very thoroughly and cut them on the bias to form elongated slices.

Ingredients:
- 1 2.2-lb/1-kg guinea hen
- 1¾ oz/50 g salt pork
- 4 large leeks
- ⅓ cup/80 ml cooking oil
- 3½ tbsp/50 g butter
- 3 carrots
- 2 onions
- 1 cube chicken bouillon
- 2 sprigs of tarragon leaves, roughly shredded
- 1 bunch of chives, chopped finely
- salt and pepper

Serves 4
Preparation time: 15 minutes
Cooking time: 40 minutes
Difficulty: ✳

2. Heat some oil in a roasting pan. Season the bird with salt and pepper and butter it. Roast in a medium oven for 35 to 40 minutes.

The guinea hen is a native of Africa where wild varieties continue to exist. It was much appreciated by the Romans who called it the "hen of Numidia" or the "hen of Carthage." Today this exotic fowl has become a domesticated fixture of the farmyard, but it has not lost its wonderful succulence.

Though more flavorful and original than ordinary chicken, the guinea hen has the same simplicity. You can accomplish this delectable dish with little work and no difficulty. Or, if you prefer, you can substitute rabbit as the central element.

Frequent basting is the key to success in this recipe, as otherwise the meat will dry out. Serve this aromatic dish very hot. Also, it can be reheated at any time without loss of flavor or quality. So rejoice! Here is a fowl dressed up in its Sunday best; it will appear on the seventh day and sing its blessings at your table.

Our wine expert warns that tarragon, an inveterate philanderer, tends to "undress" any wine. So choose a young vintage that can put up some resistance to its impertinence, a Saint-Émilion, for example.

3. Melt a tablespoon of butter in a heavy deep pan. Add the leeks and sprinkle with salt. Add water just to cover the leeks and cook over low heat for 8 to 12 minutes.

4. Peel the carrots and onions and chop them coarsely. Dice the salt pork.

Hen with Tarragon

5. After 35 minutes, remove the hen from the oven and pour most of the fat from the pan. Add the diced onions, carrots and salt pork to the pan, stir, and return to the oven. Reduce the oven heat and continue roasting for 5 or 10 minutes, then take the pan from the oven and remove the bird; keep warm.

6. On the stovetop, deglaze the pan with the bouillon. Reduce it by half, strain through a fine sieve, and reheat. Off the heat, swirl the remaining butter into the sauce and add the tarragon leaves. Arrange the leeks on a platter, place the bird on them, and nap with sauce. Garnish with the chives and serve immediately.

Young Pigeons with

1. Clean the pigeons; remove the legs and bone the thighs. Fold flesh and skin of the thighs down over the leg bone and tie in a rounded "ham" shape. Skin and fillet the breasts; set aside. Crush the remaining bones and carcass. Coarsely chop the onion and carrot.

2. Brown the crushed bones and carcasses in oil in a heavy deep pan. Add the bouquet garni and chopped vegetables, stir, and brown briefly. Add the white wine and enough water to cover. Season with salt and pepper and simmer for 30 minutes.

Ingredients:
3 young pigeons
1 onion; 1 carrot
6½ tbsp/100 ml cooking oil
1 glass white wine
1 generous lb/500 g girolles or other wild mushrooms
3½ tbsp/50 g butter
1 cube chicken bouillon or 1 cup/250 ml pigeon stock (see basic recipe)
6½ tbsp/100 ml heavy cream
1 pint red currants
1 bouquet garni
2 sprigs chervil
salt and pepper

Serves 3
Preparation time: 1 hour 10 minutes
Cooking time: 1 hour
Difficulty: ☆

Breasts of fowl of any kind are delicate, tender pieces which lend themselves to stylish presentations. But the flesh of young pigeons is especially exquisite since the birds have hardly ever flown. These *suprêmes*—a term originally used for the white meat of fowl, and later extended to the fillet of any small game animal or fish—are morsels that well deserve their name.

Follow the chef's directions carefully in forming the leg pieces into the shape of "little hams." It is the sort of whimsical touch that makes French cuisine so special. This operation requires a bit of skill, but it is fun to do and well worth the trouble when you think of the polish and delight it lends to the final presentation.

Reserve the bones of the little birds to form the base of the sauce. Add a *brunoise*—chopped onions and carrots, seasoned with thyme and bay leaf and browned in butter. This particular combination of vegetables and herbs is at the base of virtually every meal prepared in a French kitchen, be it humble or grand. When these ingredients are cooked, reduced and strained, you will have a typically French sauce: concentrated, flavorful, and exceptionally refined.

These *suprêmes* of young pigeon merit a place at the highest tables, and you can trust this dish to make the most important meal a success. To seal the elegance of the occasion, toast your special guests with a fine wine, a Latour 64.

3. Clean the girolles or mushrooms carefully. Fry them in butter in a frying pan. Season with salt and pepper.

4. Season the portions of pigeon. Heat a little oil and butter in a pan, and sauté the breast and thigh pieces.

Red Currants and Girolles

5. Set the pigeon pieces aside and keep them warm. Pour off the fat, and deglaze the pan with the strained pigeon stock, or with a bouillon cube dissolved in 1 cup/250 ml water. Add ¾ of the girolles to the broth and stew over very low heat.

6. Blend the sauce thoroughly with a hand-mixer. Stir in the cream and let thicken over low heat. Adjust the seasoning. Just before serving swirl in bits of butter. Spoon sauce onto a serving platter and arrange the pigeon on it. Garnish with the fresh mushrooms, red currants, and chervil. Serve very hot with the sauce.

1. Clean, singe and quarter the chicken.

Ingredients:
1 plump corn-fed
 chicken
6½ tbsp/100 g butter
3½ tbsp/50 ml
 cooking oil
1 bunch small new
 carrots
1 bunch small spring
 turnips
10½ oz/300 g fresh
 green beans
10½ oz/300 g
 mushrooms
juice of 1 lemon
2 cups/500 ml crème
 fraîche
salt and pepper

Serves 4
Preparation time: 35 minutes
Cooking time: 30 minutes
Difficulty: ☆

2. In a deep heavy pan, brown the chicken pieces in a little butter and oil. Peel the carrots and turnips and carve them into rounded shapes corresponding to their natural contours. String the beans, and cut the mushrooms into quarters.

Here is a proud hen who, like any aristocrat, is equally at ease in the town or the country. Start the cooking at a high heat so the bird browns well. Remember that using a combination of oil and butter when browning prevents the butter from burning and possibly spoiling the dish.

To ensure lightness in the final dish, pour the fat from the pan when finished browning the poultry and before deglazing with the mushrooms' cooking juices. Allow the liquid to reduce to one-fourth of its initial volume so that the chicken will be imbued with the flavor of the mushrooms.

Fresh, young vegetables are the obvious choice to compliment the finesse of this chicken. Bright and crisp, they will dress up this pretty coquette.

Aromatic to the extreme, this succulent chicken will fulfill its promise of happiness for the palates of your guests. They will not fail to delight in this feast.

Our wine expert, a true connoisseur, affirms that the elegance of a great Moulin-à-Vent (Georges Dubœuf) will guarantee the success of this fine dinner.

3. In a saucepan cook the mushrooms in 1 tbsp butter, the lemon juice, and a glass of water. Salt lightly. In separate pots of salted water, poach the carrots, turnips and green beans, being careful to keep them crisp. Pour off the mushroom broth and reserve.

4. Once the chicken is golden brown, pour off the fat. Pour in the mushroom cooking juices, cover, and simmer the chicken very gently for 20 minutes.

Village Hen

5. Stir in the crème fraîche, season with salt and pepper, cover and allow to cook 10 minutes more over low heat.

6. Just before serving adjust the seasoning and, reserving several pieces of each sort, add the poached vegetables to the chicken and sauce. Stir gently and briefly simmer, then place the vegetables and chicken on a serving platter. Finely strain the sauce and spoon it on. Garnish with the reserved vegetables.

Leg of Lamb

Ingredients:
1 leg of lamb weighing
    4½ lbs/2 kg
4 cloves of garlic
oil
several anchovy fillets
4 tomatoes
4 lamb kidneys
1 cube veal bouillon
butter
1 generous lb/500 g
    puff pastry (see
    basic recipe)
1 egg
thyme
salt and white pepper

Serves 8
Preparation time: 25 minutes
Cooking time: 40 minutes
Difficulty: ✶✶

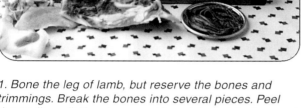

1. Bone the leg of lamb, but reserve the bones and trimmings. Break the bones into several pieces. Peel the garlic, split the cloves and insert them into the meat with the sharp point of a knife.

2. Season the meat with salt and pepper, heat a large oven-proof dish and brown the leg well on all sides in a little oil. Add the bones to the pan and roast the lamb for about 15 minutes, or until ¾ done, in a hot oven. Remove it from the oven and let cool.

The culinary style called *Arlésienne* refers to a typically Provençal preparation of local products, often calling for anchovies.

The best lamb is milk-fed, from a young animal that has not been weaned and never grazed. Nourished with its mother's milk, it has an extremely delicate flesh. To avoid any problems with boning the leg of lamb, ask your butcher to do it for you.

The puff pastry traps all the aromas and flavors inside its golden crust, and delivers its secrets only at the moment of its unsealing. The lamb must be three-quarters cooked before it is wrapped in the pastry, as the crust cooks very quickly.

The kidneys and tomatoes should be prepared in separate pans to prevent the latter from disintegrating. The anchovies must be chopped extremely finely so that they completely disappear into the dish.

Profoundly Provençal, this dish richly perfumes the air while cooking. If lamb with garlic is a classic combination, the anchovy brings it a bracing whiff of the sea. The brio of this accent will lift the lamb roast to unsurpassed heights Accompany this very special leg of lamb with small spring vegetables cooked briefly in butter, an artichoke mousseline or purée, or even a succulent asparagus gratin. This brilliant gourmet presentation is as suitable for a family reunion as for the drama of a prestigious banquet. Our wine expert proposes a great classic in honor of this dish, an exceptional Château Lynch-Bages (Pauillac).

3. Dice the anchovies as finely as possible. Clean and seed the tomatoes, then cut them and the kidneys into small dice.

4. In a frying pan containing oil, sear the kidneys. Season with salt and pepper. In another pan, heat the tomatoes very lightly until just wilted.

Arlésienne

5. Dissolve the bouillon cube in ¾ cup/200 ml water. Pour off the fat from the roasting pan, deglaze it with the bouillon, and reduce it by one half. Strain the sauce through a sieve and set aside. Roll out the prepared puff pastry evenly.

6. Once the meat is cooled rub the surface with ground thyme. Wrap the lamb in the pastry, brush with beaten egg, and roast in a medium oven for about 20 minutes. Bring the reduced meat juices to a boil and add pepper. Incorporate the kidneys, tomatoes, and anchovies. Serve the sauce alongside the lamb.

Beef Fillet with

Ingredients:
4 7-oz/200-g
   tournedos of beef
   fillet
12 pieces marrow
14 oz/400 g shallots
3¼ cups/750 ml red
   wine
2 tbsp sugar
6½ tbsp/100 g butter
1 cube beef bouillon
1 bouquet garni
crushed pepper
4 sprigs chervil
coarse salt
salt and pepper

Serves 4
Preparation time: 20 minutes
Cooking time: 35 minutes
Difficulty: ✶

1. Set aside 2 shallots, and peel the rest. Bring a saucepan full of water to a boil. Blanch the peeled shallots for 2 minutes, then drain. Add the sugar to half of the red wine and simmer the shallots in it until the liquid becomes syrupy.

The fillet is the lumbar muscle which runs along the backbone and contains the most tender morsels of meat in an animal, but please note: The fillet is therefore weak in flavor. Forms of preparations that enhance or add flavors are therefore particularly well-suited to this cut of meat.

The fillet is low in fat and recommended for weight-watchers. It is rich in phosphorus, potassium, and Vitamin B-3.

To make the caramelized shallot accompaniment, the chef recommends reducing the sugared wine to the point that it becomes a syrup.

Serve this dish very hot, perhaps with new potatoes. It does not take well to reheating, so plan to prepare only what can be eaten at one meal.

This is a good choice for friends you might want to impress with your culinary skills. And this same recipe can also be used with duck.

You need to balance the sweetness of the caramelized shallots in your choice of wines: a noble red from the Margaux vineyards, for example. Our wine expert draws on her vast store of knowledge and invites you to serve a Château Lascombes.

2. Peel the remaining shallots, mince them finely and sauté gently in a saucepan with butter. Add the bouquet garni and crushed pepper, and continue to cook briefly.

3. Pour the rest of the red wine into the saucepan with the shallots. Reduce briefly. Dissolve the bouillon cube in ⅔ cup/150 ml water, and add it to the saucepan. Bring to a boil, then simmer over low heat for about 15 minutes.

4. Slice the marrow into disks, and soak them in ice water for about 20 minutes. Poach them in lightly salted water. Using a mixer, thoroughly blend the wine and stock mixture.

Caramelized Shallots

5. Remove the shallots from the syrup and set them aside. Add the syrup to the wine and stock. Enrich the sauce by swirling in half the remaining butter. Season with salt and pepper if necessary.

6. Sauté the medallions in the remaining butter. Season with salt and pepper. Place each medallion on an individual serving dish and spoon on some of the sauce. Garnish with caramelized shallots, slices of marrow, and a sprig of chervil. Add a pinch of coarse salt and serve immediately.

Quail in Pastry

1. To make the mousse, dice the chicken breast and grind it in a food processor. Refrigerate for 10 minutes. Add 1 egg, salt and pepper lightly, and process thoroughly. Add the cream, process again for a minute, and set the chicken mousse aside in a cold place.

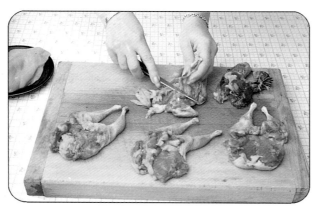

2. Using a small sharp knife, cut carefully through the back of each quail, opening out the cavity. Remove all bones except for the drumstick, leaving the flesh intact as far as possible.

Ingredients:

For the mousse:
1 chicken breast
1 egg
3½ tbsp/50 ml light
 cream

4 quail
1 cube chicken
 bouillon
1 shallot
½ cup/120 g butter
1 small can truffles in
 their juice
14 oz/400 g puff
 pastry (see basic
 recipe)
1 egg
salt and pepper

Serves 4
Preparation time: 40 minutes
Cooking time: 35 minutes
Difficulty: ✳✳

The first truffles, those "Epicurean poems dressed in black jackets", do not appear before December. Fortunately, gourmet groceries can supply them in canned form, enabling us to enjoy their divine aromas and mysterious, unequaled savor year round. Brillat-Savarin, the father of all gourmets, gave the truffle perhaps its greatest endorsement : "Its scent and the pleasure it gives to the touch are troubling and aphrodisiac."

Explore fine gastronomy by conjuring quails *en croûte*, delicate birds in shells of puff pastry garnished with the apotheosis of culinary luxury, black truffles.

Puff pastry is not easy to handle; it is not uncommon for this capricious dough to rise unevenly, or even refuse to rise at all. To avoid these problems, the chef advises that cold dough will be more stable. So, stay close to your refrigerator! Chill the dough before and after manipulating it and your pastry will rise reliably. In case of a setback, do not despair. A few flicks of the wrist can restore the dough's elasticity, but this is an acquired skill that calls for experience.

A successful mousse also requires starting with very cold ingredients, and the order for incorporating them is crucial. These are imperatives you ignore at your peril!

To add a crowning touch to these pastries, decorate their tops with incised designs made with the point of a knife.

This stylish tour de force, served with a tangy salad of field salad, will honor your most distinguished guests. Serve a Côtes-du-Rhône with this superb dish.

3. Dissolve the bouillon cube in ¾ cup/200 ml water. Chop the shallot and sauté it briefly in some of the butter. Pour in the bouillon and the truffle juice, reserving the truffles. Over low heat, allow the liquid to reduce briefly.

4. In a frying pan, brown the quail briskly in butter, sautéing them 2 minutes on each side. Season lightly with salt and pepper. Remove the quail from the pan, and allow them to cool completely. Prepare the puff pastry.

with Truffle Juice

5. Roll out the chilled pastry dough and cut it into 8 circles sized to line small tart pans. Lay a circle in each of the pans, place a bird inside, and cover with a spoonful of the chicken mousse. Brush the edges of the pastry with beaten egg.

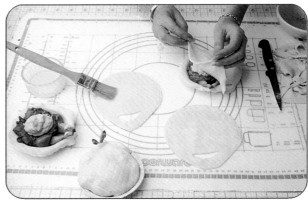

6. Leaving a vent for the protruding drumsticks, fit another pastry circle over the tart. Seal the pastries and brush the tops with beaten egg. Bake 20-25 minutes in a medium oven. Before serving, swirl 3½ tbsp butter into the sauce (Step 3). Spoon it onto a platter, arrange the pastries on top, and garnish with the truffles.

Veal Fillet with Sweet

Ingredients:
1 veal fillet of
   superior quality
1 14-oz/400-g veal
   sweetbread
6½ tbsp/100 ml white
   vinegar
flour for dredging
1 small jar capers
⅔ cup/150 ml heavy
   cream
6½ tbsp/100 g butter
½ glass white wine
salt and pepper

Serves 4
Preparation time: 30 minutes
Cooking time: 45 minutes
Difficulty: ✷✷

1. Poach the cleaned sweetbreads for 20 minutes in salted water with a bit of the vinegar; rinse. Allow to cool, then slice and dredge in flour. Cut the veal into 4 thick medallions and brown in butter; add salt and pepper. Add the sweetbread and brown on both sides.

2. Remove the sweetbreads and veal from the pan and pour off the fat. deglaze the pan with half the brine from the jar of capers. Pour in the white wine and half the vinegar, and allow to reduce briefly. This will form the base of a brown sauce.

The French name of this recipe—*veau aux capucines*—recalls both nasturtiums and the children's game "Ring Around the Rosy." Our recipe calls not for nasturtium blossoms, which are often served in salads or used to decorate platters, but for the tiny buds or soft seeds of these plants preserved in a vinegar brine—commonly known as capers. Thus, in English or in French, the fillet and kidneys of veal dance together on your platter!

Capers stimulate the taste buds, and their use is no longer reserved to fish dishes. Their tartness awakens the restrained flavors of some dishes, and lightens others. To better titillate the taste buds, our chef recommends the finer quality "little capers."

The sweetbreads must be soaked at least two hours in cold water. Change the water often, then rinse the sweetbreads thoroughly under cold running water. The addition of white vinegar to the water will prevent shrinkage and keep the color from fading.

Those who are fond of organ meats can also incorporate a veal kidney into the dish. Cook it only to the rare stage, and slice it before serving.

Young zucchini or fresh noodles will make a delicious accompaniment to this preparation. And for the final touch, why not garnish the dish with lovely and edible nasturtiums? This pair of delicate and tender meats, escorted by the pretty flowers that are akin to their French name, lets this special feasts blossom with a touch of spring.

Our wine expert suggests a Riesling du Pfersieberg Paul Ginglinger.

3. For the white cream sauce, reduce the other half of the liquid from the capers in a saucepan. Add the cream, salt lightly, and reduce briefly.

4. Incorporate the capers into the white cream sauce.

breads in Caper Sauce

5. Pour off half of the broth made in Step 2 and reserve. Enrich the remaining broth by swirling in pieces of butter. Set this pan gravy aside, and keep warm.

6. Add the reserved brown broth to the white cream sauce and swirl in the remaining butter. Adjust the seasoning. Place the medallions on a serving platter and surround with the sweetbread slices . Spoon the brown sauce onto the veal and the white sauce with capers over the sweetbread. Serve very hot.

Pigeon

1. Remove the head and claws of the lobster; cut the head in two. Bone the pigeons, reserving the carcass.

Ingredients:
1 1½-lb/750-g lobster
2 14-oz/400-g
    pigeons
6½ tbsp/100 ml
    cognac
2 shallots
1 onion
2 carrots
1 cube fish bouillon
thyme
bay leaf
6½ tbsp/100 ml
    cooking oil
¼ cup/60 g butter
salt and pepper

Serves 4
Preparation time: 45 minutes
Cooking time: 50 minutes
Difficulty: ✲✲

2. Poach the lobster tail and claws only until the shells turn pink. Remove from the water, let cool, and carefully remove the shells without tearing the flesh. Set both meat and shells aside. Peel and coarsely chop the vegetables, then brown in oil until golden.

Here we have an uncommon union which is not only original but surprisingly delicious. Alternating pigeon and lobster slices will allow you to have fun reconstituting a wing on the platter; this makes a great impression on guests. To create a complete *plat de résistance* for a special occasion, you might prepare a second lobster for the platter, as shown in the accompanying picture.

Follow the directions carefully to avoid any drying out of the lobster. Removing the flesh from the claws and tails of the lobster requires a most delicate touch in order to keep the flesh intact. You can easily substitute sweetbread or another fowl for the pigeon, taking care, of course, to cook them appropriately.

With its elements of sea, earth and sky, this recipe symbolizes the soul of Brittany, whose spirit will imbue your cooking with its scents. To prepare its food, to savor its essential aromas, to partake of its typical dishes—these are agreeable ways to approach the history and life of a province old in tradition. Prepare this for your most distinguished guests— connoisseurs of the liberal arts who know how to eat as well!

Our wine expert chooses a great white wine whose bouquet hints of tiny white blossoms. It will be the perfect arbiter between the pigeon and the lobster: Savennières Clos-de-la-Coulée-de-Serrant.

3. Crush the lobster shell and the pigeon bones. Add them to the vegetables and let them color up together.

4. Flambé this mixture with ¾ of the cognac. Dissolve the fish bouillon cube in 4 cups/1 liter of water, and add to the pot. Add the thyme and the bay leaf, season with salt and pepper, and simmer gently for 30 minutes.

with Lobster

5. Strain the broth through a fine sieve and allow to reduce over low heat.

6. Brown the pigeon in oil and butter; salt and pepper. Scallop the lobster tail and pigeon breasts into slices of the same thickness and arrange on a platter. Pour off the fat from the frying pan, deglaze it with the rest of the cognac, add the broth, and swirl in butter. Spoon the sauce over the meats and serve very hot.

Rabbit Haunches

1. Remove the bones from the rabbit, keeping the haunches and the back. Marinate these in a mixture of the onion, garlic, carrot, thyme, bay leaf, white pepper, salt and red wine. Marinate for at least 24 hours.

2. Brown the bones and the vegetables from the marinade in a saucepan with a little oil. Dissolve the bouillon cube in ⅔ cup/150 ml water and add it to the bones. Pour in the wine from the marinade. Cook until you have a full-flavored sauce.

Ingredients:

2 legs of rabbit with
   the back
1 onion
5 cloves of garlic
1 carrot
thyme
bay leaf
1½ tbsp/15 g coarsely
   ground white
   peppercorns
4 cups/1 liter full-
   bodied red wine
6½ tbsp/100 ml oil
1 cube chicken
   bouillon
5 tbsp/70 g butter
2 tbsp honey
⅔ cup/150 ml vinegar
salt and pepper

Serves 4
Preparation time: 20 minutes
Cooking time: 30 minutes
Difficulty: ✷
Marinating time: 24 hours

This marinade is a veritable magic philtre. It will give the rabbit an unexpected and delicious flavor of game. After the rabbit has finished marinating, drain it thoroughly: It will be so saturated with wine that it could boil instead of browning nicely.

When adding the honey to the saucepan, which has been drained of fat, carefully scrape the cooking juices stuck to the sides into the mixture, as they will give the sauce a full-bodied flavor. Let the honey caramelize slightly to give the sauce a glossy consistency.

A small piece of advice from our chef: If you want the sauce to be perfectly smooth, strain it through a cloth after putting it through the sieve.

This dish can be accompanied by fresh pasta or potato cakes.

Chicken, guinea-hen, beef fillet—this recipe full of autumn warmth can easily be adapted if you want some variation.

You can be confident that the gastronomic art displayed in this recipe will transform an everyday meat into rare and exquisite game. Marinades are able to dress the most innocuous of meats in a royal garb, so accompany this young rabbit disguised as venison with a fine Cornas from the banks of the Rhône.

3. Season the back and legs of the rabbit with salt and pepper, and fry them in a saucepan with a little butter and oil.

4. When the legs and back of the rabbit are done, remove them from the saucepan and keep warm. Skim away the fat from the pan, stir in the honey and allow it to caramelize slightly. Strain the rabbit stock through a fine sieve and cook until it thickens slightly.

Marinated à la Venison

5. Add the vinegar and boil for 2 or 3 minutes to let the acidity evaporate.

6. Pour in the rabbit stock, cook over low heat for 15 minutes, then strain through a sieve. Finish the sauce by whisking in the remaining butter. Place the rabbit on a warm platter and pour the sauce over it. Serve hot, accompanied by noodles.

Veal Medallions with

1. Poach the scampi in the court-bouillon; reserve the bouillon. Cut the tails from 8 of the scampi, remove the flesh, and set aside the tail meat; reserve the carapaces. Leaving the remaining 8 scampi whole, remove the shell only from their tail sections.

2. Clean and trim the veal fillet, and cut it into medallions. Peel the shallot and chop it finely. Brown the veal in a deep pan with a little oil. Pour off the fat, and sauté the shallot lightly in the same pan.

3. Dissolve the bouillon cube in 6 ½ tbsp/100 ml water and add to the shallots. Pour in ⅔ cup/150 ml of the court-bouillon and the Noilly Prat, and reduce over low heat.

Ingredients:
1 fillet of veal,
　1 lb 5 oz/600 g
16 red-clawed scampi
8 cups/2 liters court-
　bouillon (see basic
　recipe)
1 shallot
3½ tbsp/50 ml cooking oil
1 cube veal bouillon
¾ cup/200 ml Noilly Prat
　(white vermouth)
2 young zucchini
2 carrots
2 tbsp/30 g butter
1 pinch of saffron
whole blades of chive
1 sprig of parsley
salt and pepper

Serves 4
Preparation time: 20 minutes
Cooking time: 25 minutes
Difficulty: ✳✳

These succulent combination of veal fillet and crayfish is a pleasure for the eyes. While much of its beauty depends on the dexterity of the cook, if you follow these directions your success is almost guaranteed.

Let's start with the scampi: Ideally, they should be purchased live. Only so can you to be sure they are completely fresh, and that you will be able to remove the central vein easily. Once the heads and torsos are separated from the tails (on half of the scampi), it will also be easy to disengage the flesh of the tail section.

With the veal, be sure to pour off the fat after sautéing before deglazing the pan. This keeps the dish light and digestible.

Any white meat is suitable for use in this recipe, so there are many possible variations.

To provide a pretty accent for the dish, make zucchini spirals. Slice thinly through the cylinder, stopping within an eigth of an inch of the lower edge. Then, turn the vegetable over, and press with your palm slightly but evenly against the lower, uncut side of the zucchini. It will then form a spiral of overlapping petals.

You can be absolutely certain that this recipe will be a sensational success—a thrill for gourmets and esthetes alike.

Veal and scampi can be compared to star-struck lovers, and they will find a superb matchmaker in a Puligny-Montrachet.

4. Incorporate the saffron and simmer briefly. Strain this liquid through a fine sieve and set it aside.

Crayfish and Saffron

5. Trim the zucchini into sections 5 or 6 inches in length, and poach them very briefly. Slice or carve them to form spirals. Carve the carrots into elongated ovals with beveled edges.

6. Enrich the saffron sauce by swirling in butter. Place the medallions and tail meat on a platter and spoon on the sauce. Arrange the scampi, carrots and zucchini spirals artfully on the platter. Garnish with parsley and whole blades of chive, and serve hot.

1. Peel and finely mince 1 shallot. Brown lightly in a deep heavy pan with a little butter, a sprig of thyme and a bay leaf. Add the red wine and simmer over low heat. Clean the pigeon, reserving the liver. Truss the bird and roast until rare in an ovenproof dish.

2. Bone the partially roasted pigeon, keeping the legs intact. With a pastry brush, coat the legs with mustard, then bread them.

Pigeon

Ingredients:
1 pigeon
1 poultry liver
2 shallots
4½ tbsp/70 g butter
1 cup/250 ml red wine
bread crumbs
1 cube veal bouillon
2 carrots
1 stalk celery
3½ tbsp/50 ml cognac
1 clove of garlic
3½ oz/50 g girolles or wild
   mushrooms
6 tiny cream onions
thyme, bay leaf, mustard
1 sprig of parsley
salt and pepper

Serves 1
Preparation time: 35 minutes
Cooking time: 25 minutes
Difficulty: ✳✳

This authentic recipe from the area around the northern French city of Rouen was originally used in preparing duck. In this version, part of its originality arises from the breading of the leg portions, but not the breast pieces. Our chef wanted to give pigeon a chance to excel, and you will see that his variation results in savory fare, indeed.

Be sure to flambé the wine so that its acidity does not overwhelm the flavor of the sauce. The liver is another element that demands a light hand; too much blood or heaviness will adversely affect the sauce.

If you want a light-colored breading, make it yourself from bread crumbs. The commercial varieties will add color.

Eat heartily without restraint! Because of the liver it contains, the sauce must not be allowed to boil, and thus the dish does not take to reheating. You will find that a pigeon per person is a modest portion, and your diners will finish every last delicious crumb.

Heed our wine expert, master of her art, and serve an Aloxe Corton. The fruitiness and elegance of this Côte du Beaune know no peer.

3. Reduce the wine by half, add the bouillon cube dissolved in ¾ cup/200 ml water, and continue to simmer over low heat. Crush the pigeon carcass and brown it on top of the stove in the roasting dish in which the bird was baked.

4. Coarsely chop the second shallot, carrots and celery. Add these to the roasting pan. Pour in the cognac and flambé the pan. Add the minced garlic and the parsley.

Rouennaise

5. Clean the mushrooms and sauté them in a little butter until brown. To complete the sauce, pour the stock from Step 3 into the roasting pan, simmer for 15 minutes, and strain through a fine sieve. Return the legs to the oven for 10 minutes.

6. Clean and boil the onions. Clean the fowl livers, poach briefly, and grind in a blender. Add the strained stock to the blender and mix. Reheat the sauce briefly, swirl in bits of butter, and adjust the seasoning. Place the legs on a plate, nap with the sauce, and serve with parsley-strewn onions and mushrooms.

Country-Style

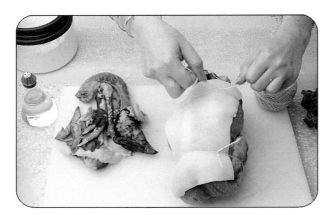

1. Clean and prepare the guinea hen. Season it inside and out with salt and pepper, wrap it in a thin layer of fatback, tie it, and lightly oil its surface.

2. Brown the wrapped hen in a deep-sided pan. Peel and finely chop the onions, garlic and parsley. Clean and trim the livers and chop them along with the ham.

Ingredients:
1 plump guinea hen
1 sheet fatback or
   desalted bacon
4 chicken livers
1 large slice prosciutto or
   dry-cured ham
1 tbsp oil
3 onions
2 cloves garlic
1 bunch parsley
5 tbsp/75 g butter
1¼ cup/300 ml white wine
1 tbsp juniper berries
1 bunch of parsley
5 tsp/25 g *beurre manié*
4 slices stale whole-grain
   bread
chervil
 salt and pepper

Serves 4
Preparation time: 45 minutes
Cooking time: 50 minutes
Difficulty: ✶

To ensure that the bird remains tender and succulent, make sure to select a young hen, though pheasant is an excellent substitute for the Guinea hen. When cleaning the livers, which are incorporated in the stuffing, be careful to remove the spleen and extraneous matter to prevent any bitterness from spoiling the dish. The livers should not be cooked beyond the rare stage, or they will harden.

The juniper berries make this recipe special. Their peppery and lightly resinous flavor add a unique aroma. Their use in cooking goes back to prehistoric times. Our remote ancestors discovered the antiseptic properties of juniper, and burned branches to cleanse the air of cave dwellings. In the Middle Ages, the curative powers of juniper were applied as a panacea for headaches and problems of the kidneys and bladder. In the French province of Dauphiné, juniper is still considered to bring good luck, and its branches are traditionally put into the bed of newlyweds.

Our dietitian points out the many advantages of this preparation: The livers make the dish rich in vitamin D, and the onions and parsley supply vitamin C.

After a day spent outdoors, the bracing evening air will put you in the mood for a solid supper. Fried potatoes make a fine accompaniment for this rustic dish, and its country heartiness will fulfill the promises of the aroma it spreads through the house.

Now is the time, too, to fetch the bottles out from behind the wood-pile in the cellar. Our wine expert suggests a Madiran or a Cahors.

3. In a frying pan, sauté all the chopped ingredients in the butter. When lightly browned, transfer half of this mixture to the pan with the guinea hen. Pour in the white wine and 6½ tbsp/100 ml water, then add the juniper berries and bouquet garni. Simmer for 30 minutes.

4. Remove the hen and set it aside. Strain the contents of the pan through a fine sieve, pressing well to extract the juices.

Guinea Hen

5. Bind the juices with beurre manié (see glossary). Discard the fatback, and divide the bird into 4 pieces.

6. Fry the bread slices in butter in another frying pan, and spread them with the remaining chopped mixture from Step 3. Place a piece of hen on each of the slices, nap on the sauce, and garnish with a few sprigs of chervil.

Leg of Mutton

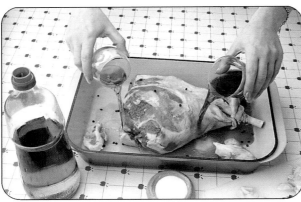

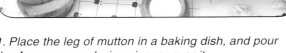

1. Place the leg of mutton in a baking dish, and pour the Armagnac and wine vinegar over it.

Ingredients:
- 1 4-lb/1.8-kg leg of mutton
- 2 tbsp/30 ml Armagnac
- 1 liqueur glass wine vinegar
- 1 bouquet garni
- 4 shallots
- 2 cloves garlic
- ¾ cup/200 ml Gamay
- ¾ cup/200 ml olive oil
- 4 tsp/20 g butter
- 2½ tbsp/20 g flour
- salt and pepper

Serves 8
Preparation time: 20 minutes
Cooking time: 25 minutes
Difficulty: ✳

2. Chop the shallots and garlic and add to the marinade with the bouquet garni. Liberally salt and pepper, pour in the wine and olive oil, and leave to marinate for 24 hours, turning the meat over from time to time.

A leg of mutton is a quality meat most often reserved for family celebrations or elegant dinner parties. Interestingly, the *gigue*, an old musical instrument, derived its name from the French word for a leg of mutton, *gigot*, because it had the same shape as the hindquarter of a sheep or lamb. This meat is fatty and full of protein, phosphorus and vitamin B.

While the meat is marinating, it should be rotated several times. This will ensure that the mutton is completely impregnated with flavor, giving this tasty, tender meat a new and subtle savor. Basting the meat with the marinade during cooking will permit it to continue its work.

If you wish you can use beef instead of mutton as a delicious variant.

Serve this dish hot accompanied by celery purée—a divine combination. It should be eaten immediately, as reheating mutton causes it to lose its tenderness.

This recipe is very simple. If you put your whole heart into it, you will introduce your guests to new, voluptuous gastronomic delights.

Our wine expert recommends a Gamay de Savoie. But if you prefer your wine a little less strong, a full-bodied Morgon would also be a fine choice.

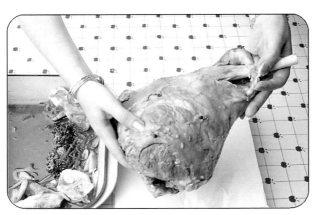

3. Drain the mutton. Remove the marinade from the baking dish and reserve it. Adjust the seasoning of the meat and roast in a very hot oven.

4. When the mutton is done, remove it from the oven. The degree to which it is cooked can vary according to taste. Pour the marinade into the baking dish. Return it to the oven for several minutes to thicken the marinade.

Marinated in Gamay

5. When this gravy is ready, work the butter and flour into a paste (beurre manié) and use it to bind the sauce. Mix well, then strain through a fine sieve.

6. Cut the mutton into slices, arrange on a serving platter, and serve it accompanied by the gravy.

Veal Sauté

Ingredients:
2½ lbs/1.2 kg boned
  breast of veal
3 large shallots
4 limes
3½ tbsp/50 g butter
2 tbsp flour
3 lemons
3 cups/750 ml dry
  white wine
6 egg yolks
1 cup/250 ml crème
  fraîche
salt and pepper

Serves 6
Preparation time: 35 minutes
Cooking time: 45 minutes
Difficulty: ✷

1. Peel and finely chop the shallots. Cut the veal breast into 2 in/5 cm cubes. Peel the limes down to the pulp and finely sliver the peel. Slice the lime flesh into crescents. Blanch the lime zest in 2 or 3 changes of water and set aside.

Limes are both more highly flavored and juicier than lemons. Therefore the lime pulp at the heart of this recipe will bring to this very simple dish a delightful tartness, agreeably suggestive of warmer climates, and supplying the tonic effect of Vitamin C.

Veal is the least fatty of meats. It of course contains protein, and is richer in iron and phosphorus than any other meat. White, sweet, very mild in flavor, it lends itself to the delicate citrus sharpness of the lime, which highlights its flavor.

As usual, discard the cooking fat after browning the meat, since it is indigestible. Let the sauce simmer for 10 minutes before adding the egg-yolk mixture, and be sure to remove it from the heat as soon as it starts to bubble. It must not be allowed to boil!

Serve this uniquely-flavored sauté with Creole rice, and invite your guests to a culinary exploration of the tropics.

Our wine expert favors a Riesling. The possibly acid overtones of the lime will be mitigated by this great Alsatian white wine.

2. Sauté the veal in a deep heavy pan containing butter, stirring frequently to prevent the meat cubes from browning.

3. Discard the cooking fat and return the veal to the pan. Sprinkle the pieces with flour and cook an additional 1 or 2 minutes.

4. Squeeze the lemons, adding their juice to the veal. Stir in the wine and simmer gently for 30 minutes.

with Limes

5. Stir the egg yolks into the crème fraîche, whisking vigorously until well combined. Add salt and pepper.

6. Stir the crème fraîche mixture into the pan with the veal. Bring it just to the simmering point, then remove it from the heat. Serve very hot, topped with the blanched lime zest, sliced lime segments, and sprigs of parsley.

Pigeon with Foie

Ingredients:
4 pigeons
10½ oz/300 g *crépine*
  (pork caul)
7 oz/200 g foie gras
flour for dredging
1 truffle
2 tbsp butter
3½ tbsp/50 ml oil
1 cube veal bouillon
2.2 lbs/1 kg fava
  beans
1¾ lbs/800 g potatoes
1 tbsp potato starch
salt and pepper

Serves 4
Preparation time: 35 minutes
Cooking time: 45 minutes
Difficulty: ✷✷

1. Slice ¾ of the foie gras, season with salt and pepper, dredge in flour, and sauté gently. Clean and mince half the truffle. Bone the pigeons, reserving the livers. Distribute the browned foie gras and the truffle on the opened birds. Salt and pepper the cavities.

For this regional dish the chef has singled out pigeons from the Bresse region of France because they are the finest available. So search out birds that are fresh and plump, if you want to bring out the full possibilities of this recipe.

The chef recommends cooking the bird only to a rare stage—always the preferred degree of doneness for gourmets. The prescribed *crépine*, or pork caul, serves to retain the meat's juices and prevent it from drying out.

Begin browning the pigeons on the breast side, as that is the side that will be visible on the serving platter.

You will note that the foie gras is floured before sautéing; this prevents it from crumbling in the pan. And remember to save some of the foie gras to enrich the sauce—provided some greedy gourmand hasn't already gobbled it up!

There is no need for worry if the sauce should cool down, as it is just as delicious cold. This delectable method of preparation, which is also suitable for spring chickens or quail, takes a little time to prepare, but that is the only reproach one can level at it. You are going to serve your guests a simply marvelous feast, one well worth the extra bit of patience it requires.

Uncork a Volnay Champans—reported to be a favorite wine of many women!

2. Close the body cavity of the bird by folding over the flaps of flesh. Re-form the shape of the birds by wrapping them in pieces of crépine. Season with salt and pepper.

3. Brown the pigeons in a heavy pan with a little butter and oil. When the pigeons are nearly done, crumble the rest of the foie gras into the pan, and add the chopped livers. Allow to cook for a short while longer.

4. Remove the pigeons from the pan and pour off the fat. Dissolve the bouillon cube in ¾ cup/200 ml water, add it to the pan, and allow the broth to simmer until its volume is reduced by half.

Gras and Fava Beans

5. Poach the beans and remove their skins. Peel and dice the potatoes, then sauté in a frying pan with oil and a little butter. When they are well-browned, add the fava beans, and season with salt and pepper.

6. Pour the broth into a saucepan and blend thoroughly to incorporate the foie gras. Bind the sauce lightly with the potato flour. Slice the remaining truffle and add to the sauce. Arrange the pigeons on a serving platter. Spoon on the sauce and garnish with mounds of diced potatoes and fava beans. Serve immediately.

Chicken

1. Clean and prepare the chicken. Soak the bladder in water containing a little vinegar, then wash it and scrub it well with coarse salt. Place the truffle inside the bird; season with salt and pepper.

Ingredients:
1 3-lb/1.4 kg chicken
1 pork bladder
1 tbsp/15 ml vinegar
1 truffle and its juices
1 cube chicken
  bouillon
2 tbsp/30 ml cognac
¼ cup/60 ml Madeira
4 carrots
4 turnips
4 potatoes
1 handful string beans
8¾ oz/250 g baby
  peas
coarse salt
salt and pepper

Serves 4
Preparation time: 20 minutes
Cooking time: 1 hour 20 minutes
Difficulty: ✶✶

2. Dissolve the bouillon cube in 6½ tbsp/100 ml water. Truss the bird firmly and carefully place it in the bladder, breast side up to avoid scarring the meat. Pour the truffle juice, cognac, Madeira and half the bouillon into the bladder. Add more salt and pepper.

The chicken featured in this recipe—*une poularde*—is a rare bird today. Traditionally, these are young fowl fattened indoors, almost in the dark. Such fowl may still be found at specialized chicken farms or gourmet grocers in France. A first-rate free-range chicken is an excellent alternative.

In this method of preparation, perfected by our chef's father expressly for the International Exposition of 1937, this fine bird is simmered (in French, "smothered") inside a pork bladder *chemise*, or shirt, yielding a surprisingly subtle taste. The aromas of truffle, cognac, Madeira and bouillon, along with those of the chicken, produce an incomparable sauce layered with flavors.

Remove the chicken feet at the drumstick joint (leaving the rounded end intact) and the wing tips, leaving the rest to tuck under before trussing the fowl very firmly. A tight, rounded bundle is easier to enclose in the pork bladder (a veal bladder can also be used.) It is advised to have an extra bladder handy in case the first is accidentally torn.

The cooking must be extremely slow in barely simmering water. Actual bubbling or boiling must be avoided to keep the envelope intact and the meat succulent; the chef recommends piercing the bladder to prevent it from bursting. When it comes time to serve this spectacular dish, press the air out of the bladder before removing the chicken. Our wine expert suggests a Moulin-à-Vent, the marvelous Beaujolais recognized for being a good companion to poultry.

3. Tie the bladder shut, first as close as possible to the body of the chicken and then again, further up.

4. Bring a deep pot of water to a boil and place the chicken in it. Use a needle to puncture the bladder. Allow the chicken to simmer very slowly, without the liquid reaching a boil, for 1 hour.

en Chemise

5. Peel and carve the carrots, turnips and potatoes into ovoid shapes. String the beans, and shell the peas, if necessary.

6. Poach the vegetables in separate pots of salted water. Place the chicken en chemise on the serving platter and surround it by the vegetables. To serve, open the bladder and retrieve the juices from the interior.

Chicken Breasts

Ingredients:
4 chicken breasts
1 generous lb/500 g pumpkin
6½ tbsp/100 g butter
4 cups/1 liter white stock (see basic recipe)
14 oz/400 g ravioli
salt and pepper

Serves 4
Preparation time: 20 minutes
Cooking time: 20 minutes
Difficulty: ✳✳

1. Peel the pumpkin and cut most of it into thin rectangular slices. Form the rest into little marbles with a small melon-ball scoop.

2. Poach the pumpkin balls in lightly salted water. Refresh them in cold water, drain, and set aside.

Pumpkin belongs to the squash family, and some varieties can weigh more than 200 pounds. Its pulp ranges from yellow to orange, and is rich in potassium, but low in calories. As a vegetable, it is a flavorful and colorful accompaniment to chicken.

Pumpkin appears on the market from October to December, and can be kept, uncut, all winter long. If none is available, you could substitute Jerusalem artichoke for pumpkin in this recipe.

The preparation of this dish presents no problems. The chef recommends that you be careful not to overcook the chicken breasts. To keep them tender and moist, poach them for only a few minutes. The white meat of chicken is the most digestible part of the bird as it has practically no fat content.

This dish should be served hot, immediately after it has cooked. But to make your task easier and allow you to visit with your guests before the meal, prepare it in advance and reheat it just before the meal. Rustic and golden, it will bring sunshine to the winter table. Our wine expert recommends a Moulin-à-Vent, the most complete of the Beaujolais range. It never fails to rise to the occasion when paired with a fine fowl.

3. Fry the pumpkin slices in a pan with a little butter. Season lightly with salt and pepper, and set aside.

4. Bring the stock to a boil, add the chicken breasts, and poach them in the simmering broth them for 10 minutes. When cooked, remove the chicken and keep warm.

with Pumpkin

5. Bring 8 cups/2 liters of lightly salted water to a boil. Cook the ravioli in it, drain them, and set aside.

6. Reduce the chicken broth to ¼ its initial volume. Thinly slice the chicken breasts and arrange them on a platter alternating with the fried pumpkin and ravioli. Enrich the reduced broth by swirling in the remaining butter. Spoon the sauce over the platter, garnish with the pumpkin balls, and serve hot.

Lobster Bisque

1. Clean or peel and coarsley chop the vegetables; peel and dice the tomatoes. Separate the head and tail of the lobster. Split the head open and break the claws. Fry the lobster pieces in the very hot oil. Add the vegetables to the pot and brown briefly. Flambé the pan with the cognac, then add the tomatoes.

2. Bring the fish stock to a boil. Stir in the tomato paste and white wine; season with salt and pepper. Add the bouquet garni and cloves and simmer briefly. Pour the stock into the pot with the lobster, and top off water to cover. Simmer for about 30 minutes. Blend the butter and flour to make a beurre manié.

3. Remove the lobster meat, strain the broth through a fine sieve, and stir in the beurre manié. Return to the heat, blend in the crème fraîche, and simmer until thickened. Adjust the seasoning and serve garnished with sliced lobster meat.

Ingredients:
1 live 14-oz/400-g lobster
1 leek
1 onion
2 carrots
1 celery stalk
2 cloves of garlic
2 tomatoes
3½ tbsp/50 ml oil
3½ tbsp/50 ml cognac
2 cups/500 ml fish stock or
   1 cube bouillon
1 tbsp tomato paste
¾ cup/200 ml white wine
1 bouquet garni
whole cloves
¾ cup/200 ml crème fraîche
1 tbsp butter
1 tbsp flour
salt and peppercorns

Preparation time: 30 minutes
Cooking time: 35 minutes
Difficulty: ✳ ✳

In current practice, "bisque" refers to a smooth, self-flavored sauce—traditionally a creamy broth of lobster, although scampi, crabs, crayfish, or any crustacean can successfully be used as the basis for this bisque.

Lobster bisque is refined, aristocratic fare suitable for festive occasions or for special guests able to appreciate gourmet presentations of high quality. It is likely to remain at the top of any first-rate menu for a very long time. This is reason enough to devote your most careful attention to producing this infinitely delicate treat for the sensitive palate.

Start with a live lobster to ensure that the flesh will be firm and the flavor superior.

The preparation of lobster bisque requires careful attention. It must be subtly seasoned, not excessively, but with finesse. Your signature on this demanding culinary work of art will surely earn you a super cordon bleu, the coveted distinction reserved for the very highest cuisine of France.

Court-Bouillon (With Lobster)

Ingredients:
1 lobster
For the bouillon:
2 carrots
1 leek
1 celery stalk
1 onion
1 shallot
whole cloves
2 cloves of garlic
1 bouquet garni
tarragon
rosemary
6½ tbsp/100 ml white wine
coarse salt and
   peppercorns

Preparation time: 15 minutes
Cooking time: 15 minutes
Difficulty: ✳

1. Peel and carefully clean all the vegetables. Stud the shallot with cloves; slice the other vegetables finely. Place the vegetables in a large pot filled with water. Add the bouquet garni, some tarragon, and a sprig of fresh rosemary.

2. Pour in the white wine and bring to a boil. Season with coarse salt and pepper and allow to simmer for 10 minutes, then strain and cool.

Court-bouillon is a spiced and aromatic stock most often used in the cooking of fish or crustaceans, but it can also be used to prepare light meats or white organ meats.

The basic preparation involves adding carrots, quartered onions (one or two of which can be studded with a few whole cloves), a bouquet garni and coarse salt to a pot of water.

The court-bouillon may also be prepared with white wine, the juice of two lemons or even white vinegar, which may be added at the end of the cooking process. After simmering to extract the flavors of the ingredients, the court-bouillon should be strained, cooled, and then reheated as a broth for the preparation of the fish, lobster, or other main ingredient.

3. For a lobster: Immerse the crustacean in the court-bouillon before or after straining, according to personal preference, and simmer for 15 minutes. Remove and drain. The lobster is ready to eat.

Gnocchi Dough

Ingredients:

4 cups/1 liter milk
2 generous cups/250 g fine
   wheat semolina
2 tsp/10 g butter
4 eggs
1 pinch of salt

Preparation time: 5 minutes
Cooking time: 20 minutes
Difficulty: ✶ ✶

1. Bring the milk to a boil in a deep heavy pan. Sprinkle in the semolina, stirring constantly with a wooden spoon. Cook on low until the mixture is completely uniform in consistency and very thick. Remove from heat, add salt and butter, and continue stirring.

2. When the dough has cooled somewhat, incorporate the eggs one by one. Heat briefly. Turn the gnocchi dough onto a buttered or dampened board (or a piece of plastic wrap) and spread to a uniform thickness of about ⅜ in/1 cm. Allow to cool.

Gnocchi can be prepared from a number of different ingredients, including f lour, semolina, potatoes, or even puff pastry. Shaped into small balls, gnocchi are normally poached, then either baked *au gratin* with a topping of shredded cheese or bead crumbs or coated with a flavorful sauce.

Originally an Italian dish, gnocchi appear under various names in Austro-Hungarian as well as Alsatian cuisine. Here we offer *gnocchi à la Romaine*, or Roman style.

The milk must be boiling when you add the wheat semolina, and this mixture must be stirred constantly. It must be allowed to cool before the eggs should be added, one by one, or they will cook!

Gnocchi are remarkably versatile: they can be made in any shape you desire and prepared *au gratin*—just bake in a moderate oven until the topping is bubbly and finish off under the grill—or fried and used as a garnish, or prepared Roman style, as described below. These are just a few examples; feel free to experiment!

3. Cut the gnocchi into shapes with a knife or cookie-cutter. For gnocchi à la Romaine, fry them in butter, turning until they are golden on both sides. Serve with tomato sauce.

Puff Pastry

Ingredients:
2½ lbs/1.3 kg cake flour
4 generous cups/1 kg
  butter
2 tbsp/35 g salt
2 cups/500 ml ice-cold
  water
flour for the work surface

1. Blend 2 ½ cups/300 g flour into all but 6½ tbsp/100 g of the butter and refrigerate. Mound the remaining flour, make a well in its center and place the salt, reserved butter, and a little ice-cold water in it. Begin to knead with the fingertips, adding just enough water to yield a pliable paste. Refrigerate for 30 minutes.

Preparation time: 1 hour 30 minutes
Cooking time: 20 minutes
Chilling time: 2 hours
Difficulty: ✷ ✷ ✷

The ideal surface for making puff pastry is a marble countertop or cutting board, especially in the summer months when the pastry must be kept as cold as possible.

Though puff pastry can be temperamental and requires a certain touch, if you follow these directions closely, your pastry is sure to be a success.

The dough must be made quickly and kneaded firmly, yet with a light touch to retain the air pockets that give puff pastry its characteristic layers. Keep the pastry as cold as possible, and work it with your fingertips.

When all the flour has been incorporated, form the dough into a ball and make a few cuts in it to allow air to circulate. Refrigerate in between steps.

When you have created your masterpiece, brush the outer layer of pastry with beaten egg before baking to give it a golden sheen.

2. Working quickly, roll the dough into a wide rectangle. Place the butter and flour mixture in its center. Fold the pastry over the butter mixture. Carefully, again roll out the pastry into a long rectangular strip. Fold in thirds with the ends overlapping in the middle. This is 1 "turn" of the dough. Repeat the process 2 more times.

3. Refrigerate the dough for 1 hour. Remove it and perform 4 more turns. Refrigerate again, and finish with 6 additional turns. The pastry is now ready to be used in any way you like.

Sauce Périgueux

Ingredients:
2 shallots
½ tsp butter
1 truffle
⅔ cup/150 ml port
3½ tbsp/50 ml cognac
2 cups/500 ml meat stock
  (see basic recipe)
6½ tbsp/100 ml truffle juice
2¾ oz/80 g foie gras

Preparation time: 15 minutes
Cooking time: 30 minutes
Difficulty: ✳✳

1. Peel and finely chop the shallots, then brown them slightly in a saucepan with the butter. Mince the truffle. Pour the port and cognac onto the shallots and reduce the liquid by half.

Périgord is traditionally one of the best locations for finding truffles, and indeed home to the finest there are: black with a subtle white grain. It is therefore natural that this recipe should bear the name of the capital city of the region, as this sauce contains both chopped truffle and truffle juice. This great culinary classic, one to be reserved for special occasions, is also called *sauce à la périgourdine*.

You can use Madeira, but port and cognac will provide more flavor and add to the delights of this sauce.

Sauce Périgueux should be served separately as an accompaniment to meat, poultry and game. It also goes well with eggs, making them something quite extraordinary.

Enjoy this delicacy, one that will add its smooth mellowness and prestige to your table.

2. Add the meat stock and truffle juice and simmer for about 20 minutes over very low heat.

3. Strain the sauce through a fine sieve and stir in the chopped truffle. Heat gently for several minutes. When ready to serve, add the foie gras cut into small cubes, and pour in a little more cognac. Simmer briefly until the foie gras binds the sauce, and serve.

Madeira Sauce

1. Peel and finely mince the shallots. Sauté until golden brown in 1 tbsp of the butter. Stir in the Madeira and simmer until reduced by half.

Ingredients:
2 shallots
3½ tbsp/50 g butter
⅔ cup/150 ml Madeira
2 cups/500 ml meat stock
   (see basic recipe)
salt and pepper

Preparation time: 5 minutes
Cooking time: 15 minutes
Difficulty: *

2. Pour in the meat stock and simmer slowly over medium heat for another 15 minutes. Strain the sauce through a fine sieve.

This delicately flavored sauce will enhance any meat dish with a subtle flavor. Guests will appreciate your special efforts as they enjoy this original and flavorful sauce.
Madeira sauce is easily prepared, yet it will give you a reputation worthy of a great cordon bleu chef. Its secret lies in the successful combination of spices, meat, and wine.
Truly a bouquet of aromas for the palate, this succulent sauce is sure to become a fixture of your cuisine.

3. Reheat the sauce for a few minutes. Just before serving, remove from the heat and swirl or whisk in the rest of the chilled butter in small pieces.

Meat Stock

1. Fry the meat trimmings in a saucepan with very hot oil. Brown well. Clean, peel and chop the carrots, onions, celery and garlic. Add them to the meat and continue to cook.

Ingredients:
10½ oz/300 g beef
    trimmings
10½ oz/300 g veal
    trimmings
3½ tbsp/50 ml tbsp oil
2 carrots
2 onions
1 celery stalk
3 cloves of garlic
2 tomatoes
1 tbsp flour
whole cloves
1 bouquet garni
1 tbsp tomato paste
salt and pepper

Preparation time: 20 minutes
Cooking time: 1 hour 30 minutes
Difficulty: ✶

2. Peel, seed and dice the tomatoes. Sprinkle flour into the mixture of meat and vegetables and mix well. Add the tomatoes, salt and pepper, then the cloves and bouquet garni. Stir in the tomato paste. Mix well and add plenty of water. Simmer for about 1½ hours over very low heat.

The simplest way to make meat stock is to fry beef and veal trimmings over high heat. When they are well browned, add the chopped vegetables, which are then cooked along with the meat. Skim off the fat before adding the fresh tomatoes and tomato paste, then liberally add water. Simmer this mixture for 1½ to 2 hours.

Strain the liquid through a fine sieve, and you will have an excellent and versatile meat stock that can be combined with a little *beurre manié* (see glossary) if you wish to make a Périgueux or Madeira sauce. You can also sprinkle a spoonful of flour into the stock after the meat and vegetables are cooked and the fat is skimmed off; this alone will make an excellent basis for a sauce. For a sauce to accompany game, add about 1¾ cups/400 ml of red wine, and reduce as desired.

3. Once cooked, strain the meat stock through a fine sieve. Reduce briefly, then put it aside for later use.

Duck or Pigeon Stock

Ingredients:
1 duck or 3 pigeons
2 carrots
2 onions
1 celery stalk
2 cloves of garlic
1 bouquet garni
whole cloves
2 tomatoes
1 cube chicken bouillon
6½ tbsp/100 ml white wine
  (for duck)
6½ tbsp /100 ml red wine
  (for pigeon)
3½ tbsp/50 ml oil
salt and pepper

Preparation time: 20 minutes
Cooking time: 40 minutes
Difficulty: ✳

1. Singe, clean and bone the fowl, reserving the meat for another recipe. Clean, pare, and dice the carrots, onions, celery and garlic. In a heavy pot, sear the duck carcass or the pigeon bones in hot oil until they are well-browned.

Traditionally duck or pigeon stock was prepared after browning the whole fowl. Then the *mirepoix*—a mixture of diced vegetables including onions, carrots and others and browned in butter—was added for flavor. The fat was poured off, and the pan deglazed with water. Herbs, cloves, salt, and pepper were added, and the stock was left to slowly simmer.

Today, it is more often the case that only selected pieces of the bird, notably the breast, are called for in recipes. This means that you need to ask your butcher for the trimmings, carcass and bones from the fowl to use in preparing the stock.

To extract the maximum flavor, crush the bones and carcass, and brown them well in very hot oil along with the trimmings.

2. When the bones are quite brown, add the mirepoix, bouquet garni, and cloves. Season with salt and pepper and add the peeled, seeded and diced tomato. Pour in the wine and continue cooking until the vegetables begin to take on color and soften.

3. Dissolve the bouillon cube in 4 cups/1 liter hot water and pour it over the ingredients in the pot. Simmer for 40 minutes. Strain the stock through a fine sieve. The stock is now ready to use.

Pork Stock

Ingredients:
10½ oz/300 g pork
trimmings and bones
3½ tbsp/50 ml oil
2 carrots
2 onions
1 celery stalk
1 bouquet garni
whole cloves
1 tomato
2 cloves of garlic
6½ tbsp/100 ml white wine
1 cube chicken bouillon
salt and pepper

Preparation time: 10 minutes
Cooking time: 40 minutes
Difficulty: ✳

1. Chop the trimmings and crush any bones, then sear them in a heavy pan with the oil. Clean, peel and coarsely chop the vegetables. When the trimmings are well browned, add the vegetables, bouquet garni, and cloves. Stir to combine and continue to cook until the vegetables color up and begin to soften.

For a cook, meat stock corresponds to a foundation for everything else. This pork stock is very flavorful and takes less time to make than more traditional preparations. Moreover, it is light and adds a delicious aroma to any dish it accompanies.

Traditionally, when entire joints of meat were roasted, the fat was poured off, the pan was deglazed with water, and chopped vegetables were added. Stock prepared in this manner cooked for only about 15 minutes.

Today cooking large roasts is less common, and modern recipes call for boned and trimmed meats. So although modern practice turns to these bones and trimmings to flavor the stock, the principle remains the same.

2. Cut the tomato into pieces and add it to the pan along with the garlic. Pour in the wine and dissolve the bouillon cube in 4 cups/1 liter water.

3. Add the bouillon to the broth, season with salt and pepper, allow to simmer for 30 to 40 minutes, and strain. The stock is ready to use.

Poultry Stock

Ingredients:
1 chicken
2 carrots
2 onions
2 leeks
1 celery stalk
2 cloves of garlic
1 cup/250 ml white wine
1 bouquet garni
3 whole cloves
salt and peppercorns

1. Clean, pare, and coarsely chop all vegetables. If necessary, singe and clean the chicken; truss it with string. Blanch the chicken in water, and place the vegetables in a heavy deep pot of salted water.

Preparation time: 15 minutes
Cooking time: 1 hour 30 minutes
Difficulty: ✶

2. Add the blanched chicken to the pot with the vegetables. Season generously with salt and pepper and add the cloves.

Poultry stock is, technically speaking, a well-flavored reduction prepared from the broth produced by a chicken cooked in water. It is used to add flavor to a wide range of sauces and soups. The art involved in its preparation lies in the regulation of the temperature of the liquids during the cooking process.

By following this recipe carefully you will be justly rewarded with a flavorful stock that will lend an extraordinary aroma to the dishes prepared with it.

The best poultry stock is drawn from older chickens or roosters. For a clear and digestible stock, skim it carefully and often, and completely remove the fat before using it.

3. Pour in the white wine and simmer for 1½ hours, skimming the fat from the surface occasionally. Strain the stock through a fine sieve before using.

White Stock

Ingredients:

1 lb/500 g veal trimmings and/or poultry giblets
2 onions
2 cloves of garlic
1 shallot
4 whole cloves
2 leeks
2 carrots
1 celery stalk
1 bouquet garni
¾ cup/200 ml white wine
salt and peppercorns

Preparation time: 15 minutes
Cooking time: 1 hour
Difficulty: *

1. Blanch the trimmings or giblets, starting with cold water. Bring to a boil, drain, refresh under cold water, and set aside. Peel the onions and garlic; stud the shallots with cloves. Split the leeks, and coarsely chop the carrots, celery, and onions. In a large pot, cover the vegetables with cold water and add the bouquet garni.

2. Add the blanched veal to the vegetables, or if using poultry, add the vegetables to the blanched giblets. Season with salt, add the white wine and peppercorns, and simmer for about 40 minutes.

A white stock base is made from poultry or veal. The process is slightly different if you are using poultry giblets: Begin by blanching them as described, always starting with cold water. Bring the water to a boil and skim off the foam frequently. When the foam disappears, instead of draining and refreshing, simply add the vegetables and seasonings to the giblets and continue to simmer for an additional 45 minutes.

Be sure to skim off any fat that appears while the stock is cooking, as the clarity and quality of the broth depends on this step.

If the broth will not be used immediately, you can store it in the freezer. Let it cool completely before pouring it into containers.

3. When finished cooking, strain the stock through a fine sieve, and skim. It is ready to use.

The Participating Chefs

Nicolas Albano
Maître Cuisinier de France

Marc Bayon
Maître Cuisinier de France
Finaliste Meilleur Ouvrier de France

Jean-Pierre Billoux

Luce Bodinaud

Jean-Claude Bon
Maître Cuisinier de France

Jean Bordier
Maître Cuisinier de France
Meilleur Ouvrier de France

Jean-Paul Borgeot

Hubert Boudey

Maurice Brazier
Chef de Cuisine
Maître Cuisinier de France

Jacques Cagna
Maître Cuisinier de France

Claude Calas
Vice-Président des Maîtres-Artisans
Maître Artisan Cuisinier

Jacques Chibois
Chef de Cuisine

Marc Daniel
Chef de Cuisine

Alain Darc

Ginette Delaive
Commandeur des Cordon-Bleus de
France

Joseph Delphin
Maître Cuisinier de France

Francis Dulucq
Maître Cuisinier de France

Daniel Dumesnil
Chef de Cuisine
Chevalier du Merité Agricole

Sylvain Duparc
Chef de Cuisine

Maurice Dupuy

Robert Dupuy

Roland Durand
Maître Cuisinier de France
Meilleur Ouvrier de France

Odile Engel

Gilles Étéocle
Maître Cuisinier de France

Jean-François Ferrié

Charles Floccia
Diplôme de Maîtrise du Club Prosper
Montagné

Denis Franc

Jean-Maurice Gaudry
Maître Cuisinier de France

Roland Gauthier

Pierre-Jean et Jany Gleize
Maîtres Cuisiniers de France

Charles et Philippe Godard
Maîtres Cuisiniers de France

Lionel Goyard
Chef de Cuisine

Bernard Hémery

Jean-Pierre Lallement
Maître Cuisinier de France

Serge de La Rochelle

Jean-Michel Lebon

Jean Lenoir
Maître Cuisinier de France
Finaliste Meilleur Ouvrier de France

Jean Claude Linget

Bernard Mariller
Chef de Cuisine

Manuel Martinez
Chef de Cuisine
Maître Cuisinier de France
Meilleur Ouvrier de France

Paul-Louis et Michel Meissonnier
Maîtres Cuisiniers de France

Christian Métreau
Chef de Cuisine

Daniel Nachon
Chevalier de l'Ordre du Mérite

Jean-Luis Niqueux
Chef de Cuisine

Alain Nonnet
Chef de Cuisine
Maître Cuisinier de France
Finaliste Meilleur Ouvrier de France

Angelo Orilieri
Chevalier du Mérite Agricole

Claude Patry
Chef de Cuisine

Christian Ravinel
Chef de Cuisine

Michel Robert
Chef de Cuisine

Armand Roth
Chef de Cuisine

Roger Roucou
Président des Maîtres
Cuisiniers de France

Gérard Royant
Maître Cuisinier de France

Georges-Victor Schmitt
Chevalier du Mérite Agricole

Pierre Sébilleau
Chef de Cuisine

Dominique Toulousy
Maître Cuisinier de France

Gilles Tournadre

Jean Truillot
Chef de Cuisine

Jean Vettard
Maître Cuisinier de France

Pascal Vilaseca
Chef de Cuisine

Glossary

BAIN-MARIE: A gentle method of heating used to either cook food or keep cooked food warm, a bain-marie consists of a pan containing food placed inside a larger pan of warm (not boiling) water, surrounding the smaller pan with heat. Placed in an oven, a bain-marie generates steam for foods that require moist heat. Compare to double boiler.

BANYULS: A sweet fortified wine made in a place in southwestern France of the same name. Port would be an acceptable substitute if Banyuls is not available.

TO BARD: To wrap or cover meat or fish with strips of pork fat (fat back, salt pork etc.) to prevent it from drying out while cooking.

BÉCHAMEL SAUCE: A basic white sauce made by adding milk to a roux. The consistency of the sauce varies greatly depending on the proportions of butter, flour and milk used.

BEURRE MANIÉ: A paste consisting of softened butter and flour, usually in equal amounts, used to thicken sauces or soups. *Beurre manié* and roux are both thickening mixtures of butter and flour, but a roux is cooked beforehand and *beurre manié* is not.

TO BIND: Adding any of a number of substances, including flour, cornstarch, eggs, egg yolk, gelatin or cream, to a hot liquid in order to make it creamier.

TO BLANCH: Briefly immersing fruits, vegetables or variety meats (innards and extremeties) in boiling water and then in cold water to stop the cooking. This process makes it easier to remove peels and skins, rids food of impurities, and preserves the flavor and color of food before freezing.

BOUQUET GARNI: A combination of herbs either tied together or bound in cheesecloth and used to flavor soups, stews, etc. The bouquet garni is removed before serving. The classic combination of herbs is thyme, bay leaf and parsley, though myriad variations exist.

TO BRAISE: Cooking technique in which food (usually meat or vegetables) is browned, then cooked in a small amount of liquid in a covered pot over a longer period of time.

TO BROWN: To sauté a food in hot butter or oil over fairly high heat, giving a browned exterior while the interior remains tender.

CHOUX PASTRY: A simple but unique dough that is prepared on the stovetop by bringing water or milk to a boil, adding flour and then beating in several eggs to form a sticky paste. This is the classic puff pastry.

CLARIFIED BUTTER: Butter that has been melted slowly without stirring, then skimmed and decanted, leaving the milk solids and water in the pan. This liquid is pure butter fat and has a higher smoking point than whole butter, but less intense flavor.

TO CLARIFY: To remove any particles which interfere with the clear appearance of liquids (i.e. jelly or consommé), usually by straining or binding the impurities, often by adding and then straining out egg white.

CONSOMMÉ: A meat-based stock that has been reduced and clarified; it is used as the base for soups and sauces.

COULIS: A thick sauce consisting of puréed fruit, occasionally with lemon juice or sugar added.

COURT-BOUILLON: A flavorful broth made with clove-studded onion, celery, carrots, a bouquet garni, and occasionally lemon and garlic. Court-bouillon is most often used to boil different fish and meats.

CRÈME FRAÎCHE: A thickened cream with an incomparably smooth texture and nutty, not sour, taste. It is indispensable in French cuisine, particularly in sauces since it does not separate when boiled. If not readily available, crème fraîche can be simulated by adding 1tsp-1tbsp buttermilk to 1 cup heavy cream and letting the mixture stand at room temperature 8-24 hours until thickened. This will keep up to 10 days in the refrigerator.

CRÉPINE: French for pork caul, which is the inner membrane lining the animal's stomach. It is used to wrap around various sausages and meat dishes and does not need to be removed after cooking.

TO DEGLAZE: Using a liquid such as water, alcohol or stock to dissolve food particles in a pan after food has been roasted or sautéed in it. This liquid is used as the basis of the sauce which accompanies the food.

TO DEFAT OR DEGREASE: To skim or pour off the fat that results from cooking meat or soups, for example. This is often done before deglazing a cooking pan to make the sauce much lighter.

TO DICE: To cut fruit or vegetables into even, dice-like shapes. Traditional dice is between ¼ and ½ inch (.5 and 1 cm) in size.

DOUBLE BOILER: A double boiler consists of two pans that nestle into each other. The bottom pan is filled with simmering water and the top pan rests over, but not in, the hot water, providing gentle heat to melt or cook delicate foods like custards or sauces. Compare to bain-marie.

EMULSION: A combination of difficult-to-combine elements such as water and oil, achieved by adding the second ingredient a drop at a time while whipping continuously.

TO ENRICH A SAUCE: The finishing touch for many French sauces, this involves thickening and refining a sauce just before it is served by adding small pieces of very cold butter, or occasionally crème fraîche or egg yolk. This should be done off the heat, preferably by swirling the saucepan, but a whisk or wooden spoon may be used.

FATBACK: Fat from the back of a pig, used in its natural form, rather than salted or smoked. Compare to salt pork.

FILLET: Any boneless piece of meat or fish.

TO FILLET FISH: To separate the flesh of a fish from its bones to obtain fish fillets.

FINES HERBS: A mixture of finely chopped herbs, classically fresh parsley, chives, tarragon and chervil, usually added to dishes at the end of their preparation.

TO FLAMBÉ: To pour alcohol over food and light the alcohol, imparting a very special flavor. This can be a dramatic presentation or an earlier step in the cooking process.

TO GARNISH: Decorating a dish to make it more visually appealing with various edible elements; also refers to the accompaniment itself. Garnish varies from a single piece of parsley, to the additions to a soup, to entire dishes served with the main entrée.

TO JULIENNE: To slice foods, primarily vegetables, into thin, regular matchsticks; also refers to foods sliced in this way.

TO KNEAD: To thoroughly combine and work the components of a dough either by hand or with the dough hook of an electric mixer to produce a homogenous dough. It can take 15 minutes or longer to produce a smooth, elastic dough when kneading by hand.

LANGOUSTINE: Commonly, but inaccurately, called prawn, these crustaceans resemble tiny Maine lobster and are not to be confused with shrimp.

TO LINE: To cover the inside of a mold or pan with whatever ingredient is called for. For a charlotte, lady fingers would be used. For aspic, the mold would be lined with gelatin.

TO MARINATE: To soak meat, fish or other foods in a marinade (aromatic liquid) for a period of time to allow the meat or fish to develop a deeper, richer flavor and become more tender.

MELON BALLER: A special spoon shaped like a tiny bowl used to carve circles from melons and other fruits and vegetables.

MESCLUN SALAD: A mix of several varieties of young salad greens that may include radicchio, frisée, sorrel, arugula and others.

MIREPOIX: Diced combination of vegetables, usually including carrots, onions and celery, which are browned in butter and used to add flavor to stews, sauces, etc.

TO NAP: To cover food with a thin layer of its accompanying sauce.

PÂTÉ: A mixture of ground meats, pork fat, seasonings and sometimes vegetables ranging from smooth to coarse.

PINEAU: A sweet, white fortified wine made in the Cognac region of France. If this is unavailable, a mixture of grape juice and cognac may be substituted.

TO POACH: A method of cooking food by immersing it in hot, but not boiling, water or other liquid.

TO RECONSTITUTE: To add liquid to dried or dehydrated foods, such as powdered milk or dried fruits and vegetables.

TO REDUCE: The fundamental step in sauce preparation is to cook a mixture until much of the liquid has evaporated, resulting in a thicker and more intensely-flavored sauce.

TO REFRESH: A means of preventing foods from continuing to cook in their own heat either by immersing the cooking pan in cold water or running cold water directly onto the food.

TO ROAST: A slow method of cooking food uncovered in the oven, which allows tender meat or fish to brown and caramelize on the outside and remain moist on the inside.

ROUX: A combination of flour and butter used to thicken sauces. Unlike beurre manié, roux is cooked for several minutes before any liquid is added, and has different levels of readiness: light, medium and dark.

SALT PORK: Fat from the belly and sides of a pig that is cured with salt. It is often blanched to reduce its saltiness. Compare to fat back.

TO SAUTÉ: A method of cooking in a very small amount of hot oil or other fat, usually in an uncovered pan. Food may be lightly sautéed (see to brown), or cooked all the way through.

TO SCALLOP: To thinly slice meat, fish or crustaceans.

TO SEAR OR SEAL: To brown food very quickly, usually by sautéing it in pre-heated fat, so that its surface seals or locks in the food's natural juices.

TO SKIM: To remove any impurities (fat, foam) which form on the surface of a liquid.

TO STRAIN: To pour or press ingredients through a sieve or alternatively through a piece of cheesecloth in order to remove impurities, lumps, or seeds.

TO STEW: To cook by simmering food just covered in liquid for a prolonged length of time. Stew also refers to the resulting dish, which is usually savory, but can also consist of fruit.

TO SWEAT: A method of cooking vegetables, especially onions, or other ingredients over low heat in butter or oil until they are transparent, without letting them brown.

TOURNEDO: A very lean and tender cut of beef tenderloin, just 1 inch (2.5 cm) thick.

TRUFFLE JUICE: The liquid won during the process of drying the celebrated truffles. An excellent and less costly means of adding the flavor of truffles, it is available from gourmet shops. Truffle oil, high quality oil in which truffles have been steeped, is another alternative.

TO TRUSS: To sew the legs of a chicken or other bird to its body in order to preserve its shape during cooking; also used more loosely to refer to securing any meat in a compact form.

VERJUICE OR FRENCH VERJUS: A fermented liquid made from unripe fruit, usually grapes, and used in cooking.

Index of Recipes